THE NEW
DESIGN RULES

THE NEW DESIGN RULES

HOW TO DECORATE *and* RENOVATE, *from* START TO FINISH

EMILY HENDERSON

with Jessica Cumberbatch Anderson

Photographs by Sara Ligorria-Tramp
Produced and styled by Velinda Hellen

Clarkson Potter/Publishers
New York

TO ALL THE RULE BREAKERS
WHO OPENED UP THEIR HOMES
TO LET US SHARE THEIR
CREATIVITY WITH THE WORLD.
YOU INSPIRE US.

CONTENTS

INTRODUCTION

Four years ago when I pitched this idea to my editor, I had no business writing a book about renovating, despite my actual business of being an interior designer. I didn't go to design school. I'm not formally trained. And yet, this book is full of more real information, beautiful photographs of talented designers' work, practical knowledge, and applicable trade secrets than I could ever learn in school. You see, over the last ten years, since I won HGTV's *Design Star*, I put myself through a virtual design school while renovating houses on my blog, with my readers watching and waiting for the results. The pressure was intense, and the results needed to be amazing. So every day I googled "how do you design . . . fireplaces, staircases, paneling, vanities . . . " The entire time, I wished so badly that I had a guide to this incredibly intimidating and permanent decision-making process. I was a stylist. I could combine pillows and choose wallpaper faster and better than almost anyone, but renovating a home? That's a whole other beast.

Here's the truth: Every project is chockfull of its own challenges and potential mistakes, no matter how many times the house has been renovated. Because YOUR house—that is, the one in your mind's eye—has never been designed before. A formula does not exist. It's not like making lasagna from a time-tested recipe, which is sure to give you fantastic results every time. Sure, I've designed homes in the same style, but every house is different. Every decision needs to be specific to the architecture, location, function, and style of the home, and the needs of the family that lives there. What guides the design is completely personal, which means the process is emotional in every way.

Every house I've renovated has been full of successes and mistakes. Some regrets are bigger than others—and the only benefit of me making them is that I get to share them with *you* so you don't make the same mistake. And yet, all the successful decisions I've made and lessons I've learned have grown my confidence and pride in my work.

One of the most important things I've learned is that while I do get better with experience, I also find that "rules" and knowledge of "what is right" tend to restrict my creativity and quirk. No one wants to make permanent, expensive errors, but creating a generically designed home—even if it's totally functional—is the biggest mistake you can make. Chasing trends may end in regret, but chasing what everyone else is doing can end up quite boring.

I want you to make more informed choices. You should know the rules, but I want you to be able to break them with confidence. A truly custom home should be functional, but it needs to be interesting—because you, my friend, are interesting. In part one, we teach you how to speak the language of the pros you'll need to call on if DIY is not your thing, and we go through every element of a house—from window treatments to flooring

to lighting. Then in part two, we go room by room and discuss not only how that space "should" be designed, but also highlight how you might break those rules, which is not only okay but necessary. Throughout this book, you'll find gorgeous images of in-demand designers' work (see page 334 for a complete listing of everyone), as well as rooms of my own to keep you inspired.

My goal is to help you create the home that you wish a designer would have designed for you. Because you are your own best designer.

Welcome to *The New Design Rules*.

Stylist Scott Horne's dining room is a study in vintage and rustic simplicity with just the right splashes of drama thanks to the black chandelier, table lamp, and bar tray.

IT'S ABOUT TO GET REAL

There are few things more rewarding than a fresh start. When it comes to decorating, renovating, or building your own home, that start is usually the result of months—sometimes years—of mood swings, shopping sprees, and daydreaming about how your new baby is going to turn out. Come to think of it, designing is not unlike childbirth, to be honest, only with less physical pain.

But, my friends, it's worth it, I promise.

No home renovation project will ever be carefree—let's just clear that up now. You are putting your life's savings into this house, for Pete's sake, so you're going to want to make it good. *Really* good.

When it's all said and done, you'll kick back in your beautifully crafted house, soaking in and admiring your perfectly chosen bathroom fittings, and you'll forget all about those dreadful days picking out tile and mulling over the layout, color, or style of a cabinet. Like giving birth, you kinda forget the painful moments almost as soon as they're done. I call it "renovation amnesia," and getting you to a place of blissful forgetfulness is, in many ways, the goal of this book.

Before you dive headfirst into the details of a home renovation project—as tempting as that is—hit pause and do these three things first.

SET YOUR PRIORITIES. Fast, cheap, and good would be a dream way to design a home, but that trifecta is a myth. You can have fast and good, but not cheap. You can have cheap and good, but not fast; and you can have fast and cheap, but it likely won't be good. So you have to choose the two that matter the most to your unique emotional, stylistic, and financial situation.

COME TO TERMS WITH HOW MUCH YOU CAN HANDLE. A full gut reno is just that, gutting, in every sense of the word—physically, emotionally, literally, and figuratively—and it will almost certainly require you to move out of your home, displacing yourself and your family. A room-by-room reno, on the other hand, is a process that can take much more time—perhaps years. It will save you money, since you won't have to rent a temporary place to live, but that comes with its own frustrations. Whichever approach you take, remember the amnesia part. You'll forget all about it afterward, I promise.

DECIDE WHAT KIND OF HELP YOU NEED. What's the true scope of the work, and how can your stress be mitigated by bringing in a professional to do the job? I love DIY, but not everyone is cut out for it. You need to be honest about whether or not you are that person. Do you like doing it? Do you have the time? And, more importantly, are you willing to learn new skills? If the answer is no to all (heck, any) of those questions, then look at yourself in the mirror, say, "Thank you for your honesty," and give your reflection a kiss. Self-love is a big part of surviving a renovation.

Once the DIY debate is settled, you'll still need to figure out exactly what kind of project you have on your hands. Unless you're building a new home, you likely fall into one of two categories—renovations or updates—and understanding the scope of each will help you determine which one matches up with that home vision board you've been obsessing over.

YOU MIGHT BE AN UPDATER . . .

Your place needs a face-lift: a little refreshing here, some tightening there—some home Botox, so to speak. This kind of project is about enhancing the finishes, not the structure itself. Think: swapping out bathroom and kitchen hardware, adding a fresh coat of paint, or having a favorite piece of furniture reupholstered.

As an Updater, you want to transform your space without spending a ton of money, without hiring too many people, and while staying in control. Read: keeping your cool when things inevitably feel like they're spiraling out of control. These updates can add a ton of value—to your house *and* your life—and they often require only a carpenter, plumber, or electrician. But how do you do it without dipping into Renovator territory? How do you change your house without upsetting your life? I got you. Keep reading.

MAYBE YOU'RE A RENOVATOR . . .

Welcome to the big leagues. Renovating can be scary and chaotic and exciting, but there's one thing to remember: Not all renovations are created equal. No two renovations are alike, even. On one end of the spectrum, you're moving walls (or stripping them down to the studs), shifting power and plumbing lines, throwing around terms like "spatial planning," and building your dream home one layer at a time, and sometimes from scratch. The other end of the renovating spectrum isn't exactly what I'd call DIY, but it's definitely a lighter touch than a full gutting; it's what some pros refer to as a "replacement reno," in which the foundation of a room stays the same but every finish and fixture that meets the eye is, well, replaced. Where your project lands on the renovation scale all depends on (1) your budget, and (2) how compatible the bones of your home are with how you want to live.

hot tip You can be an updater and a renovator at the same time—after all, not everyone should do everything at once. To save money or to buy yourself more time while you plan a bigger project, think about how you can update one space while you're renovating another. You'll still enjoy something new in both spaces and you're less likely to make permanent decisions that you'll regret in the end.

CHOOSE YOUR PLAYERS

Next, it's time for a casting call. Unless you or your partner is a general contractor or one of those people who don't mind spending days down a YouTube rabbit hole, you're going to need some help. Here are the major players you might need to hire.

GENERAL CONTRACTOR (GC)

WHO NEEDS THEM: Renovators, updaters, new builders.

WHAT THEY DO: A GC is someone who will (or should!) manage your entire project from demolition to move-in. Their biggest responsibility is managing flow and ensuring licensing of subcontractors, or subs. They have a team of subs (framers, electricians, tile installers, plumbers, and stone fabricators, for example) at the ready. They should have expertise in how houses are built or renovated from the inside out, and they bring with them a catalog of experiences and mistakes to steer clear of with every new project.

WHERE TO FIND THEM: The best way to find a good GC is by word of mouth, truly. If that fails, use a combination of searching Google and reading reviews. As with any relationship in life, choose carefully—chemistry and reliability are *huge*—and watch out for red flags. If a GC takes a week to return an email and speed is important to you, be wary. But also, be gracious. An in-demand contractor will often be on a job site and not necessarily tethered to a mobile phone or computer. Give them a little breathing room.

HOW THEY CHARGE: GCs typically charge two ways:

- **Fixed quote per project.** For this pricing model to work, you have to clearly outline the scope of the work at the very beginning. That means knowing what tile you want for the guest bath, how the flooring will be installed, and so on. Once that's all on the table, your GC will calculate a quote based on your perfectly curated outline. Ideally, you'll get multiple quotes for the same scope of work so you can negotiate the best offer.

But even with the best-laid plans, changes will arise. GCs call these adjustments a "change order," which means that the quote is revised based on how the scope of work changes. This will hike up your price, naturally. If mistakes happen, everyone needs to be reasonable in figuring out how to fix them.

PROS: GCs are more motivated to bring on their most efficient subs and get the project done faster.

CONS: If you don't know what you want in full detail, you can rack up a hefty amount in change orders but defining the full scope up front can push back the start date.

buyer beware The lowest bid may be a sign that the GC has less comprehensive insurance coverage, or that they aren't complying with licensing standards. All of those flags could cost you more when mistakes arise.

pro tip Quality and experience are far more important than a GC's style preferences. The truth is, you may not identify with them stylistically at all. What you want from contractors is expertise, not agreement on a shade of paint or stain.

• **Time and materials.** This is a cut-and-dried pricing structure, so you can start immediately. You pay the cost of the subcontractors, plus all materials, and an additional 15 to 30 percent for the GC's expertise and management. Although it doesn't require you to know your full scope of work up front, this option can be more expensive.

PROS: You pay people their rightful rate for their work—nothing more, nothing less.

CONS: It can cost more. If they are slow and charge you by the hour . . . Well, you get it. You have to be way more on top of things and truly trust your GC.

ARCHITECTS

WHO NEEDS THEM: Renovators, new builders.

WHAT THEY DO: Calling in an architect may sound next-level, but why and when to hire one has a lot to do with your budget, the scope of the work, and frankly how daunting the major changes feel to you. Honestly, it would be awesome to have one on every job, but sometimes you just need a babysitter and not necessarily Mary Poppins. That said, if you're building a house, reconfiguring rooms, or needing expertise in style and space planning, you'll seriously want to consider hiring an architect.

These pros have expertise about how a home functions from the inside out. What matters most to them is how a house lives, breathes, and looks—before you even bring in the sofa. They'll consider the sunrise-sunset and wind pattern, for example, to ensure that you aren't putting your dining room under a window with glaring sun during the hottest time of day. They'll weigh in on flow, lighting,

hot tip Architects are the surgeons of the home design world. While all of us home design experts are subject to stereotypes, what they say about architects' strong point of view is often true. Listen to them, but be prepared to stand your ground.

air, and the innate elements that work with the style of your house.

WHERE TO FIND THEM: If you love the styles of the homes where you live, or have seen other homes whose design you're into, doing a little recon on who built those homes is a good starting point. Your local American Institute of Architects (AIA) chapter will also have a list of members to consider for your project. Or, go with a design-build firm, which typically offers both architectural design and construction services under one roof.

HOW THEY CHARGE: What you pay for an architect's services (and how) will vary widely. In some cases you'll pay hourly, a percentage of the construction cost (ballpark: 5 percent to 15 percent for new construction, and 15 percent to 20 percent for remodels), or by the square foot. Some architects do a combination of hourly fees while they're drafting plans and then charge a fixed rate once the construction phase begins.

PROJECT MANAGERS (PM)

WHO NEEDS THEM: New builders, renovators.

WHAT THEY DO: A PM does just what their title suggests: They manage the project. (If only I had one for my life!) The scope of their work covers everything from ordering materials, coordinating deliveries, keeping track of deadlines, and facilitating daily communication with the GC or subs. PMs are crucial for big jobs, like building a house from scratch, but they're also useful to have on smaller projects, too. (And yes, you can be your own project manager.)

WHERE TO FIND THEM: Many in-demand GCs will have a project manager on their staff.

HOW THEY CHARGE: PMs are typically paid a percentage of the overall project budget.

KITCHEN AND BATH DESIGNERS

WHO NEEDS THEM: New builders, renovators, updaters.

WHAT THEY DO: If you want your hardworking spaces to be more functional (and pretty), but you aren't looking to move any walls, then enlist the help of a showroom's kitchen and bath designer. These experts are incredibly smart and resourceful, know the functionality of these spaces well, and may be more enlightening and well versed than a GC about storage ideas and new tech.

WHERE TO FIND THEM: Many kitchen, tile, and plumbing showrooms function as a retail store and design center in one and will have a resident designer on hand to help you visualize what each element will look like (and how it'll function) in your space. To find a designer who isn't associated with a showroom, check out the National Kitchen and Bath Association's digital directory of pros. (Similar to architects, certified kitchen and bath designers have five years of design experience under their belt, along with knowledge of construction, mechanical, plumbing, and electrical systems. There's also an exam and ongoing rounds of professional development required to keep their certification current.) Or—always a good bet—phone a friend with a really nice kitchen and ask them who did their work.

HOW THEY CHARGE: Independent designers typically charge hourly, in addition to a consultation fee. Others charge a retainer or flat fee that includes a specific number of hours spent planning and sourcing items. Rates vary wildly, from three to five figures, depending on the level of detail and revisions needed.

HOW TO ENTER THE DIY GAME

So you want to do it yourself. Go for it!

My best advice for going the DIY route: Conserve your sanity by doing some research first. And because you're saving on labor, invest in really good materials. Here are my go-tos for a quick but high-impact home refresh:

PAINTING

A fresh coat of paint on a bland, off-white wall can completely transform a space (and bring a surprising amount of joy into your home). Most important, it doesn't cost much, and it's DIY-able. Cabinets and woodwork are trickier surfaces to paint, but they're still doable and worth every minute of extra work you'll put in (see page 224 for cabinet color ideas).

REPLACING

So the previous owner added gross lighting throughout the house. You don't need a contractor or even an electrician to replace it. Same goes for that ugly faucet—as long as you don't change the location or function, you can easily swap it out. Even replacing old flooring, carpeting, lighting finishes, and wall treatments are tasks that you can manage, no contractors required.

ENHANCING

If your walls and ceiling are blank canvases and you're handy with a drill, saw, and wood putty (or know someone who is), consider adding some simple millwork to your walls or ceiling. Applying molding or paneling (see page 149), is a very simple and easy way to add definition and depth to your rooms. A ceiling medallion for your new chandelier will really make the room.

HIRING HELP

Don't feel like hiring out is a coward's move. It's not. Here are a few people you'll want to keep on speed-dial no matter what kind of DIY project you're taking on:

HANDY PEOPLE: Handy people *love* tinkering, fixing, replacing, and solving problems, and will leave your home more updated in a matter of hours. They might charge anywhere from $35 to $60 an hour, and the superstars, like anybody, are absolutely worth it.

YOUR OWN SUBS: Wallpaper installers, refinishers, carpenters, electricians, and plumbers are all contractors you may be hiring to do updates around your house. Get multiple quotes, read reviews, look at their prior work, trust your gut.

Sometimes, though, DIY lives up to its name, and a home refresh is truly a solo job. When in doubt, start small—like with a gallon of paint and a trip to the hardware store.

rule breaker Jess Bunge hacked her rental kitchen countertops with plywood—yes, plywood, people!—added right over the top of the original counters and heavily sealed the wood and silicone around the sink to keep water out. Instead of replacing the cabinets, she simply took off the front for an elegant, open shelving look.

AVOIDING RENO REGRET

1

LIVE IN IT. Not until you actually live in the home will you realize how best to utilize different spaces and discover their functionality at different times during the day. I've renovated a home before I've lived in it and discovered that if you can hang for a couple months or at least visit the house *a lot* at different times of the day, you'll make better long-term decisions.

2

USE RESTRAINT. It's more expensive to take away than it is to add along the way. I know it feels like *right now* is the time to do something interesting, and in a way it is. But overdesigning is easy to do. Calm it down and come back to those flourishes when it's time to decorate.

3

INVESTING IN CUSTOM? MAKE IT UNIQUE. I've seen custom cabinetry and millwork that looks generic because no interesting decisions were made. Don't pay for custom if it's going to look like you got it off the shelf. It can still be simple, but make it special.

4

HAVE A CLARIFIED VISION. The more you can home in on your specific vision, and then identify the elements that you need to achieve that look, the less design regret you're likely to face down the road.

5

START WITH THE MOOD. Decide how you want a room to feel *before* you decide how you want it to look. This is crucial. To start, play with adjectives that make you smile. These could be *calm*, *exciting*, *happy*, *warm*. How do you want guests to feel when they walk into that room?

6

THINK YEAR-ROUND, NOT SEASONALLY. Well-designed decor looks right at home in the summer as well as the winter. Focus on good year-round lighting (planned and natural) and creating a transitional vibe with more permanent textiles. Try not to get caught up in the moment. Think, instead, of the things you love to live with all year long.

7

DON'T CHASE EVERY TREND. Who doesn't love a good trend? But if I could give one piece of advice it would be this: Get riskier with furniture, decor, lighting, hardware, and wall treatments (wallpaper and paint included). When it comes to hard finishes like tile, cabinets, and flooring, stick to a more timeless look that complements the architecture of the house.

8

REALITY-CHECK YOURSELF. How do you really live? Don't make decisions based on just aspirational ideas on Pinterest if they don't fit your home or lifestyle.

UPDATING A VINTAGE HOME

I think quite possibly the most controversial conversation in the design world revolves around whether or not to preserve the original integrity and charm of a vintage-style home. But we all want to make our homes reflect our style and work better for our family—so how do you renovate a home without ruining it?

When tackling a major renovation, you might be tempted to strip it all down to start over, but before you do, reference these handy rules to help you get what you want and need from your home, while giving it the respect it deserves.

Like people, with more age comes more soul, and anything vintage or antique has more depth than anything new. Not to get all woo woo on you, but the energy you get from the history, the life, of the house, cannot be duplicated (although replacing something really worn with something vintage or reclaimed does help). For anything that is salvageable—especially wood—really think about how it could be used, updated, or relocated before you replace it.

TRY TO WORK WITH IT, especially if it's high quality and still in good shape. You might be surprised at how much a coat of paint next to that vintage tile will make you fall back in love.

DON'T WASTE SPACE or "avoid a room" just to preserve something that is architecturally original. I've done this before and it's so stupid. Go ahead and take down that built-in hutch to open up the room and make your home more functional and usable for your family.

EMBRACE THE WEIRD. They don't make houses with quirks anymore, likely because those details were part of a bygone way of life, so if you have something decidedly odd about your hundred-year-old house, don't give it up so easily.

OPEN UP CHOPPED-UP ROOMS to create better flow but mimic the original architecture in the doorway openings and archways. Frame it with the same molding, millwork, trim, or shape that carries through the rest of the house. Or create a more decorative archway—something that has more of a vintage style than just a squared-off opening that could give off new-build vibes.

ASK YOURSELF if this is special or just old? If you don't like something that is falling apart or somehow impractical and is not special to the house, then brainstorm how to make that space special through new or salvaged architectural elements that might mimic the original era.

AVOID INSTALLING permanent decorative tiles or patterns that didn't exist the year the house was built. Definitely break this rule for plumbing fixtures or lighting, as it's more acceptable to update and modernize those elements in a home (and again, they can be switched out more easily than tile).

IF YOU OWN YOUR HOME, feel empowered to *own* your home. If you hate the dark stain of the millwork in your Craftsman and know you'd be happier with it painted a light color, then paint it. You shouldn't let your home hold you hostage stylistically. Either make it yours or sell it.

Despite my hoarder tendencies as a stylist, my own living room design was all about "clean, fresh, purposeful." I stayed focused on the big items—this gorgeous blue sofa from Lawson Fenning, a vintage trunk that I've had for forever, two accent chairs from Target, and an incredible reclaimed wood coffee table.

WINDOWS AND DOORS

I'll never unhear the answer "windows and doors" when I asked an architect where he would splurge in his own renovation. I thought it would be flooring, lighting, a Jacuzzi tub for his miniature schnauzer. But after going through a few renovations, I get it. These are your most visually prominent architectural features, the ones that you see and use every day. So yes, when you give them extra consideration, they can have extra impact (even in their own quiet way). They are the "smiles" and "eyes" of the home, and once you experience good-quality windows and doors, it's hard to imagine going back to your old ones or opting for cheap versions.

But don't head to Windows and Doors "R" Us and replace yours immediately. There are chic and even charming ways to break some standard rules for windows and doors and get something special without splurging.

REPLACE OR KEEP 'EM?

Windows and doors are one of the most expensive and also labor-intensive upgrades you can make, so it's not always an option to replace and upgrade them—especially all at once. When on a budget, I once updated my aluminum windows by painting the frames white instead of replacing them, and it was a great affordable fix. Here are your options:

REPLACE WITH READY-MADE. If you have a standard-size opening, you can try to just order and switch them out. Just try to match the existing ones throughout your home.

REPAIR ITS FUNCTION AND PAINT. Replace any broken glass, preferably with double-pane panels if possible. For old windows or lites (aka door windows), if the glass is in good shape, get them reglazed to help with weatherproofing (this is a straightforward DIY). Scrape, prime, and paint any exterior wood. Check out interior storm windows rather than exterior ones, which could disrupt the exterior aesthetics of your home.

REPLACE WITH CUSTOM. This could cost you anywhere from $500 to $5,000 per window and $1,500 to $20,000 per exterior door, but consider it one of those long-term home investments you shouldn't have to do again for many years to come.

BE SUSTAINABLE. Talk to your contractor about additional ways to insulate older windows to be more energy efficient without replacing them. There are UV rated films you can apply as well as weather stripping options.

ALL ABOUT DOORS

When choosing the placement and/or type of exterior and interior doors, start with how the door will function and interact with the space. Does your room have enough clearance for a door swing or could you install a pocket door instead? Do you need more privacy or could this be a good opportunity to infuse some light into a dark room?

You won't care about door size until you try to get your sofa through it. Good news: The door and sofa industries have agreed to work together (proverbially), and most sofas will fit inside a 36-inch door. But note other clearances. (Is your entry a tight hallway? Do you have low stairs?) And if you are in an older home, measure that door. Thirty-six inches has only been standard for a few decades. Here's where to start:

PICK YOUR DOOR STYLE. Research the architecture of your home and get inspired (but not confined) by what you discover.

CHOOSE THE DIRECTION OF THE SWING. Most doors swing open into rooms, not out into hallways. Doors for small closets and storage rooms tend to swing out. Exterior doors typically swing inward (for security reasons), but screen or storm doors swing out, opposite the exterior door.

SELECT THE MATERIAL. Choose from wood, glass, fiberglass, or metal (wood doors are more traditional, glass can be modern, fiberglass doors are energy efficient and low maintenance, and steel doors are fireproof and very secure).

CONSIDER ADDING A DOOR CASING. You'll definitely up the architectural interest of the room by adding it, but

even more fuctionally, trim conceals unsightly gaps left between the frame and the drywall.

PAINT OR STAIN. Some real estate studies have revealed that painting your exterior door certain colors can boost your home's value. You can go as bold as bright yellow or turquoise or stick with a wood stain, navy, or black, which has the best resale value.

DEFINING THE DOOR

A LITE: The sections of glass panes in a window. A grid is the number of panes in the window, set up like a multiplication problem. When you hear something like a 2 x 3 grid, the first number references the amount of panes horizontally (2), while the second number references the amount of vertical panes (3).

B DIVIDED LITE: When you add a grid to your window, it becomes a divided lite and you count the lites to determine the layout, with the horizontal lites stated first and the vertical lites second. For example, this window is a 2 over 2 or 2 x 2, which means 2 horizontal lites and 2 vertical lites.

C CASING OR TRIM: Woodwork that surrounds the doorframe.

D PANELS: Rectangular shapes on the door that are for aesthetics.

E IN-SWING/OUT-SWING: Door that swings to the interior, or a door that swings to the exterior.

To find out whether you need a left or right swing, stand on the secure side of the door. If the hinges are to be installed on the right of the door, then the door swings left; if hinges are to go on the left, then the door swings right. If you can, it's best to order doors in person so everyone is clear on what swing you need!

SLAB VERSUS PREHUNG: A "slab" refers to just the door itself with no frame or hinges (good for customizing the frame and better to use if you have a contractor who can install); prehung is the door slab, plus the frame, hinges, and hardware, and is ready to install.

hot tip For energy efficiency while still sticking to the traditional divided lite style, opt for "simulated divided lite" which gives you the look of true divided lite but with double or triple panes.

TYPES OF DOORS

Let me show you the door—that is, a few different types you might consider installing in your home.

1 **HINGED:** Also known as a passage door, this is the most common type of interior door. It's fixed to one side of the frame and has a "swing" into the space one way or the other. Think about your furniture location and how you really walk through the house. Bedrooms tend to open into the space, but whether the door swings right or left has to do with the layout of the room (you don't want to open the door into a dresser, for instance).

2 **FRENCH:** The romantic French doors are always a classic. These double doors can have a decorative divided lite pattern or be all glass. And don't think of them just going from inside to out, they can be beautiful ways to divide a living room from a dining room while still letting light through. If you have heavy weather opt for an in-swing if you don't have an awning outside your door.

3   **SLIDING:** A great way to save space (when there's no room for a swing), the sliding door lets in light, is generally easy to operate, and allows for more flexible furniture placement. Larger sliding doors that go wall to wall can be called scenic doors and they run a pretty penny, so make sure you really need that function—sometimes a standard sliding door with flanking glass panels will do the trick.

4   **DUTCH:** Oh the charm of the Dutch door, which really channels all our dreams of a more pastoral life. The Dutch is divided so that the top functions independently from the bottom. Great for the kitchen or mudroom doors where you might want the space to feel open but still have some confinement or if you want to keep your pets (or livestock) from coming in.

5 **WALL-MOUNT SLIDING DOOR/BARN DOOR:** A great aftermarket sliding door option, especially if you can't install a pocket door. The barn door slider is installed on a visible track and can be ready made, custom, or even something salvaged. Artist Ben Mendansky saw this as a great opportunity to bring in soul through a vintage panel. Since you will see it all the time, let's make it pretty.

6 **HIDDEN DOOR:** Not every door needs to shout DOOR, especially if it's not leading to a place you need to access frequently or call out, like a door into the garage. Continuing the pink wall color and goldenrod baseboard makes this door disappear seamlessly into this room.

7

POCKET: No matter your architectural style, a pocket door is a great functional option that saves space. It operates by sliding into a pocket in the wall, allowing furniture placement to be flexible (there's no swing). Don't limit yourself to a flat panel—you can have multi-panels and even add a window into the door. Typically used for small bathrooms, pocket doors are easy to install but can't be slid into walls with electrical or plumbing so you need to plan in advance to ensure the location of your light switch doesn't conflict with your pocket door dreams.

Let the light (and looks) in. A solid front door gives more privacy, but a door lite can give you more natural light. Or think about adding a transom window (above the door) or sidelites (windows to the sides of the door) if you not only want to let in some natural light but also have more privacy.

rule breaker Sara Ruffin Costello created a secret door to the en suite bathroom out of an antique furniture piece.

LEFT: Play with styles—your doors and windows don't have to match. By using the same materials, these French doors have divided lites while the window is all glass.

WINDOWS 101

Overall, when choosing new or replacement windows for your house, it's important to first think about the architecture of your home. The look of the window will affect the exterior look-and-feel as well—and curb appeal goes a long way in the resale of your home. Secondly, consider the function of the window for each room, as well as the outside elements. Which way does the wind typically blow? Where does the sun typically shine in?

Let's take a closer look at window materials:

WOOD is the most popular material used for the window frame (on the inside, at least), as it is classic, easy to fix, beautiful, and can be painted or stained. Depending on the wood species, it can be very expensive and if you live in a moist or extreme climate, ask your salesperson for the longest lasting solution. We love windows with a wood interior and an aluminum clad exterior meant to withstand the elements for decades.

VINYL windows are cost effective as well as low maintenance. But the color can fade in extreme heat; the window would need to be replaced, since it cannot be repainted. If you have a classic or vintage home, know that vinyl can make it look cheaper, so keep them subtle and try to mimic the original window style when possible (and be wary of white simulated divided lites—where the grid is inside the glass).

FIBERGLASS is not the most common, but it is durable and low maintenance. It can look similar to a PVC frame but can be repainted. It's sound resistant, weatherproof, and an excellent insulator. But it is not a budget choice.

ABOVE: Stained glass window panels add a craftsman touch to this home.

CENTER: A gorgeous picture window frames a rain forest of tropical plants outside.

While a vintage arched window can prove to be challenging in the window treatment department, architecturally special windows like this make a house sing.

ANATOMY OF A WINDOW

A FRAME: The head, jamb, and sill make up the framework that supports the window.

B HEAD: The top horizontal section of the window frame.

C JAMBS: The vertical pieces of the frame.

D SILL: The lower part of the frame.

E SASH: The operable part of the window (both vertical and horizontal) that holds the glass in place.

F LITE: A pane of glass that is framed separately within a window. You might have a grid of lites in one window.

G CASING: The millwork that surrounds the window.

H GRILL: The strip dividing panes (divided lites) can be commonly referred to as the grid, although it can come in a diamond pattern as well.

BASIC WINDOW STYLES

There are obviously many more styles than what I've included here, but this is a roundup of the primary types of windows you'll encounter in most homes today.

1 **CASEMENT:** Versatile and energy efficient, this type of window is attached on one side of the frame with the sash swinging outward, typically with a crank handle. They're a great choice for an operable air filtration window; they can also help block wind direction. Can also be a double casement, opening from the center with a transom above or not. FYI, this means that screens are on the inside of the window and are more noticeable.

2 **PICTURE OR "FIXED" WINDOWS:** Have a pretty view and no need to open? A picture window is nonoperable and designed to fill a wall area to maximize natural light and view in a space. Plus they are more affordable since there are no working parts, and they come in all sorts of divided lite patterns, so ask your contractor if you NEED the window to function, as it's a great place to save a few hundred dollars.

3

SINGLE- OR DOUBLE-HUNG: The most traditional "looking" window is the single- or double-hung. Put plainly, these go up and down versus in and out (like the casement). A single-hung only lifts up, but a double can lift bottom-up or push top-down. They are often the same price, so opt for the double for more airflow options. An older double-hung can be drafty so think about redoing the weather stripping if you aren't replacing the window. If customizing new windows, play with the grid pattern; you can always design divided lites on top and have all glass on the bottom.

hot tip For wood windows, painting the grids a color that contrasts with the wall and trim color is a great opportunity to add some unexpected style and depth to a room.

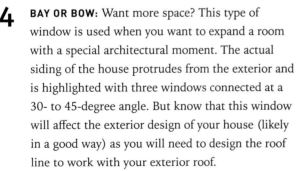

4 **BAY OR BOW:** Want more space? This type of window is used when you want to expand a room with a special architectural moment. The actual siding of the house protrudes from the exterior and is highlighted with three windows connected at a 30- to 45-degree angle. But know that this window will affect the exterior design of your house (likely in a good way) as you will need to design the roof line to work with your exterior roof.

5 **SLIDER:** A favorite of mine in a kitchen or anywhere you want to open the window quickly (such as if your fried fish strips are burning!). The slider is ideal for when the width of the window is much larger than its height. Usually fast and easy to operate, it operates side to side instead of in and out or up and down.

6 **AWNING:** Hinged at the top of the frame, this style cranks opens outward to let air in. They can be a good choice for rainy climates where they can be opened slightly for air circulation but prevent rain from streaming inside. A high horizontal window like this can also be called a transom; if above a doorway, it's called a clerestory.

be sustainable If you are replacing windows make sure you are maximizing them for light, so you don't have to turn on too many lights during the day.

A SKYLIGHT HIGHLIGHT

If you're looking for a way to boost happiness around your home, let me suggest adding a skylight. They can be installed either fixed or casement style, and anywhere with direct access to the roofline. Most are powered by solar energy (no battery replacement or electrical involved) and can be controlled via remote or smartphone. And don't worry—you have both room darkening or light filtering options for deep sleeps and bright sun.

hot tip While the terminology has changed over time and is nuanced, in general, shades go up and down, and curtains move right and left.

WINDOW TREATMENTS

When I was a stylist, I would use gaffer tape to hang curtains temporarily for catalog shoots. Not until I started designing homes for clients with real needs did I learn how to address privacy and light control through the incredibly vast world of window treatments. What the right shade can do for your room, both in function and style, is pretty special. But the world of window treatments is an intimidating one full of so many options and foreign terminology.

Quality window treatments are the central air of decorating. They're a luxury that you may feel you don't need, but when you have some that really *work,* you feel so lucky and fancy. And let's not forget how much color, texture, pattern, and warmth they can add to your home.

To start, consider your needs: Do you need light control (shades to block harsh sun throughout the day, and give you darkness at night) or privacy (to block the neighbors from peeping in)? Most window treatments automatically give you privacy (unless they are extremely sheer), so how dark you need the room to be should likely dictate your choice.

HARD WINDOW TREATMENTS

These are made of solid materials like wood, bamboo, aluminum, composite, or vinyl. They are easier to clean and therefore can be a better option for people with allergies. But they're not always hard! Shades can sometimes be made up of soft materials. My favorites include:

1 **ROLLER SHADES:** Straight-up functional, these shades are kind of like good Spanx: They should disappear and show off the goods. You can layer them with curtains to add additional light control, visual interest, and energy efficiency. Roller shades are best for large picture windows in more contemporary homes or rentals where you want to save money.

2 **CELLULAR SHADES:** This pleated or honeycomb style has a higher-end look than roller shades. You can get single-cell or multi-cell honeycomb shades, which can reduce heat loss at the window by as much as 50 percent. These are great for a contemporary style home; I have also paired them with drapery for more traditional style windows—the double function is a real crowd-pleaser.

3   **NATURAL WOVEN SHADES:** Made of a natural fiber, woven shades bring in texture without introducing another "color" to your scheme. These are found slightly more often in traditional homes and are a favorite way to add a casual, beachy, or boho vibe. There are a lot of ready-made shades available and they are way more affordable than fabric roman shades.

4   **INTERIOR SHUTTERS:** Shutters can add so much immediate charm. Christen Sacco of Custom Decorators, Inc. notes they are a much more considered choice because of the measuring and professional installation involved. Think of them as an architectural feature you're adding—they will increase the value of your home, so go for quality here.

SOFT WINDOW TREATMENTS

Being made of soft materials, these window treatments give you more options than do hard window treatments because of the almost infinite assortment of colors, patterns, and fabrics they come in. The basic styles I prefer include:

1 ROMAN SHADES: I love the clean function of roman shades in almost every style of home. They lend a softness and warmth to a room in such a streamlined way. If you know you are going to stay in your home for the long haul, they are worth the investment. There are a lot of different styles of roman shades—you can find ruffly and romantic, or a simpler flat panel, so if getting custom, be sure to explore your options.

2 CURTAINS: The most popular and easy to install, curtains are typically unlined (such as sheers), and can be shorter in length than drapery (for example, to the windowsill) and more informal in style. Before you go custom know that these days there are endless affordable ready-made options at all our favorite big box stores, both in color and pattern and with different room darkening or lined options.

3

DRAPERY: The curtain's older sister . . . or mom really, drapery is generally custom made and are thicker, more formal and often more expensive than curtains. You have plenty of lining and pleat options, and while they can be an investment, they should be a high-quality product that will last decades (so be wary of trendy patterns that you might get sick of).

YOU HAVE OPTIONS

Installing shades comes down to whether you want the shade mounted on the inside of the window frame or on the outside. Also, do you really want a cord?

INSIDE MOUNT gives you a cleaner look, but when open, the stack takes up a lot of space and will reduce your view out the window. Inside mount is a great choice for roller or cellular shades (either pleated or honeycomb) because their headrail takes up less space at the top of the window. Make sure your window has enough depth inside the top of the frame so you can fit the headrail. If you have a deep sill, consider getting the length customized to land at the sill, not spill over it, so that light doesn't leak on the sides because of the protrusion of the sill.

OUTSIDE MOUNT is more forgiving when you don't have the room for inside mount, and when you want to make your windows look taller. You can cheat the height by mounting the shade eight to ten inches above the frame and letting the fabric hang just below the bottom of the frame. Christen Sacoo recommends a two-inch overlap in width to help reduce light leakage at the sides. Opt for outside mount when installing heavier, thicker roman shades, where the stack can be six to twelve inches and block a lot of light.

CORDLESS: Unless you are good about winding the cord around the toggle thingy, the cord can dangle and tempt your cat or child to rip, pull, or cut your cord, breaking your shade and potentially harming your child or pet. Cordless shades are controlled by simply pushing them up and pulling down (via a tab). They aren't great for heavy shades, or high ceilings that will necessitate you reaching up to open the shade completely. In that case (or for the ultimate smart home) go for an automated shade that will activate with the touch of a remote or app, or at the sound of your voice.

ABOVE: Fool your eye—install shades near the ceiling even if window height is lower to make your ceilings look higher (and thus the room look bigger).

OPPOSITE: Don't need blackout shades? A lightly lined roman shade can still be shut for privacy while letting beautiful light into the room.

ABOVE LEFT: Tricky window angles (like our bay window) required two flanking smaller shades with a larger in the middle. Just know to add some breathing room between each shade so they don't slam into each other and look messy on the angle.

ABOVE RIGHT: Lining up the width of your shade to match the outside width of your window casing is a great way to have it look tailored and intentional. Here, the window and shade look perfectly integrated.

be sustainable Thick curtains and energy-efficient cellular shades (and a combo of both!) can keep in warmth in winter and keep out heat in summer, helping you greatly reduce your energy usage and your utility bills. UV-reducing films can cut down the effects of any UV damage from sunlight and save you from having to replace your textiles too often. (The films are easy to apply, but will add a green tint.)

hot tip If you have really wide windows, you might need to get four panels instead of two to have the volume you want when the curtains are both open and closed.

TREAT YOURSELF: GO CUSTOM

If your windows are irregular, if you want a color or pattern that you can't find in stores, or you simply want to rely on experts to advise and execute this for you, then consider going custom (see page 330 for Resources). I *love* working with a custom window treatment company for so many reasons.

Not only will a window treatment designer help you to get it right, but they will also give you access to more options. Your professional will come to you and guide you window by window. They'll measure your windows and bring fabrics and hardware samples to your home and help you make choices. A professional installer will do all the drilling and hanging.

But, of course, you saw this coming: Custom anything is more expensive than ready-made, and window treatments are no exception. They are expensive. According to Andy Jenkins of Decorview, custom window treatments for an average house cost $5,000 to $7,000, depending on how many treatments, how complicated they are, and the materials involved. If you can budget for it, they are a worthwhile investment for your home.

Want custom on more of a budget? All is not lost! Many online companies have sprung up to fill the demand, allowing you to choose your material online and place your order. They then sew and ship you the window treatments. You won't have an in-person expert to visit your home, but you can save about half the cost of truly custom versions.

ABOVE: Corners can be awkward, so a rod connector allows full function in a streamlined way.

OPPOSITE: A "top-down, bottom-up" shade is especially great if you live on the street level and want privacy from pedestrians or traffic, while still having the shades open to let in the light.

HOW TO HANG CURTAINS

Because hanging curtains is so easy to get wrong, I've simplified window treatment installation:

1

HANG THEM HIGH. The higher you hang the rod, the higher your ceilings will look. Install the rod a half to third of the way down from the crown molding or ceiling to the top of the window frame.

2

HANG THEM WIDE. Install the brackets of the rod at least 10 to 15 inches beyond the sides of the window frame and add at least one ring on the outside of the bracket. This will make your window look so much larger and will allow you to completely open the curtains so they don't mask the view. Note: Make sure your curtains are twice as wide as your window frame, so the panels don't look too taut and weird when closed. You can double up on panels on either side and have your tailor or dry cleaner sew them together or just hang them as is.

3

GO FOR LONGER LENGTHS. Skip the 60-, 72- and 84-inch styles unless you have really low ceilings. For the standard eight- to nine-foot ceilings, spring for the 96-inch length, hang them high, and then hem them from there. (You can even use hemming tape as a quick fix.)

4

STREAMLINE THE HARDWARE. While you want easy function, clips, exposed S hooks, and curtain tabs can look messy at the top. Opt for rod pocket-style curtains if you're shopping for ready-made—this style hides the rod. Or you can add drapery hooks to the back of the curtain top and attach them to curtain rings. Voila! You've upgraded a ready-made curtain to look more custom.

pro tip If you have wide and high windows and you want to close them off from wall to wall, have a track installed.

OPPOSITE: If you want to skip the center support bracket on a window be sure to buy light, likely unlined, curtains to avoid any rod dip.

THE PERFECT HEM

The most common curtain mistake is the too-short curtain, aka the waiting-for-a-flood curtain. It is just awkward and makes everyone uncomfortable. You have three options that will help you avoid this look:

1 **THE FLOAT:** If you want your curtains to look tailored and hang totally straight without any break at all, then the slight float is the best option for you. Hem them so they hang about a half-inch above the floor.

2 **THE PUDDLE:** Here, the drape puddles all over the floor, lending a more feminine, old-world feel. Allow an extra three to six inches of fabric to hit the floor. This is an especially good idea for thick and grand fabric—either washed linen or velvet—because the more the curtain puddles, the more you can see the beautiful texture of the fabric you probably splurged on. Avoid this look for thin cotton curtains, which will simply look way too long.

3

THE KISS: With this style, the curtains barely touch the floor. This is the hardest one to pull off, as you need to measure accurately from the rod (don't forget to include the measurements of the rings and clips or S-hooks holding your curtains). It is my favorite style, as it looks the most custom and intentional. There is often a tiny break or bend in the curtain when it's open (like a trouser break), but I'm totally okay with that.

ABOVE: A single panel is just enough curtain for a narrow window, and the addition of a roman shade offers plenty of coverage.

ABOVE RIGHT: With windows that meet in a corner, opt for a corner rod with a joining piece instead of two separate rods.

BOTTOM RIGHT: Doors don't have to be stuck with roman shades. Drapes can be great options for big doors with lots of light.

hot tip For a more traditional or custom look, add a pleat at the top but know that this will increase your "stack" on either side of the window, and unless you hang your curtains and rod very wide (as shown here) the fabric will encroach on your window, reducing your natural light.

LEFT: Rods don't have to be round: This square wood rod lends a modern feel. I love how it picks up on the wood tones elsewhere in the room.

CHOOSE YOUR FABRIC STYLE

While curtains, drapes, and shades can be found in almost every fabric, I have a few favorites—and warnings:

SHEER: Great for filtering light; they add some privacy while still letting in natural light.

LINED: A lining makes a simple curtain feel more luxurious, offering privacy and filtering some light.

BLACKOUT: Opt for room-darkening styles for most bedrooms and media rooms, especially if you take your daytime TV-binging seriously.

COLOR AND PATTERN: When determining the color and pattern of window treatments, think about whether you want them to be a huge feature of the room's design or a supporting player. If going custom, stay safe. Because they are such an investment, you don't want to tire of the pattern after a few years. An architecturally appropriate and subtle check, stripe, or small pattern can add an additional layer to the design that can make your home look extra special.

buyer beware For rooms that get blasted with sun, consider a lighter-colored fabric, because the sun will bleach the edges very quickly.

FURNITURE

Sofas and headboards and armchairs, oh my. You are drawn to pattern, color, and a cool shape—I am, too—but before you get too emotionally attached to that camelback settee, you should think about your support needs, your sitting style, and the ergonomics of the piece. Don't get me wrong: You definitely want the wow factor that a *good* collection of furniture delivers. You just don't want it at the cost of function, and certainly not comfort.

In this chapter, we'll explore the function of furniture and help you figure out the what, where, why, and how of the most important pieces in your home. Spoiler: A sofa isn't just a sofa, and the distinction between a club chair and a wingback can make a big difference to your neck. Let's go.

THE SOFA

Outfitting the living room with furniture—specifically buying a couch—is usually the first thing people think about when moving to a new place, and for good reason: We spend *so* much time here.

So how do you spot a comfortable sofa? I could toss around sofa dimension measurements all day, but finding a good couch really comes down to a few choices:

THE SIT-AND-VISIT

This sofa tends to lean more formal and, unsurprisingly, less loungeable. With a high back and a shallow seat depth (around 20 to 22 inches), it's basically designed to keep you more upright.

THE LOW-SLUNG

A really low-to-the-ground, deep-seated sofa will look more casual and make you feel more relaxed as you sink into it. The back height is low and the seat is deep, anywhere from 23 to 26 inches.

THE GOLDILOCKS

In the middle of those two is the more versatile option, and what most of us are searching for: a sofa with a modern, contemporary style, something sophisticated yet cozy. Look for a back height of 26 to 32 inches, depending on how tall you are, and a seat depth of 24 inches.

Consider your lifestyle when picking out a sofa. If you like to entertain more formally, go for the Sit-and-Visit (top); if you're a family of loungers, then embrace the Low-Slung (bottom). Or have the best of both worlds with the Goldilocks (opposite).

hot tip The softer your foam's density, the more it will compress and lower when you sit down, so take this into consideration when choosing your cushion construction and preferred seat height.

CUSHIONS 101

Another way to think about which size sofa you need is by how many people it will need to accommodate every day. One cushion per person will give you the roomiest fit, especially if you're lounger/sprawler types. But cushion count is also a matter of aesthetics.

SINGLE CUSHION: A "bench seat" is a great option for fitting as many people as possible on a sofa, with no one stuck in the crack of two cushions. With just one cushion, the sofa has a cleaner and more modern look, but that also means that you only have *one* chance to flip the cushion and hide that red wine stain. Aesthetically, though, I *love* a single cushion.

MULTIPLE CUSHIONS: Having more seat cushions translates to a roomy seat for two or more, but can be awkward for the person stuck in the middle of two cushions. The more cushions you have, the busier-looking and more traditional.

TIGHT BACK: Just like it sounds, tight back sofa cushions are built into the frame (and sometimes tufted) for the most tailored look and some extra seat depth to scooch back while sitting.

LOOSE BACK: If you drool at the thought of sinking into a sofa and being enveloped in the cushions, then a loose back style is the way to go. The look leans more cottage or Shabby Chic and will require a fair amount of flipping and fluffing to keep it looking new. But fiber or down alternative filling are an easy way to minimize that.

STRETCH OUT WITH A SECTIONAL

Want to level-up the comfort? Opt for a sectional. They tend to bring a more casual vibe to the space. Here are some common configurations:

1 **L-SHAPE:** With two sofas merged together at the end to form a right angle, the L-shape design is the most versatile of sectionals, working well wedged into a corner or floating in the middle of a room.

2 **CHAISE:** Think of it as the simplified cousin of the L-shape sectional with an attached ottoman that can go just about anywhere a conventional sofa might go.

3 **U-SHAPE:** If you have a huge space to fill, the U-shape style is for you. What's more, it's perfect for fostering intimate conversation, thanks to its two extended arms, which face each other.

4 **MODULAR:** Like flexibility and playing with blocks? This "selectional" can be reconfigured based on your needs. They usually sit lower and are designed in the postmodern style (think: 1970s and 1980s).

CHARS

The living room chair is the fastest way to make a timeless, if not basic, sofa look cool—by giving it some cool friends.

1 ARMCHAIR: Simply a chair with wooden arms, versus a club chair, which often has upholstered arms. They're a great way to add wood or another material to your room without sacrificing comfort.

2 BARREL CHAIR: Named for its barrel-like design, it has a rounded back that comes along the sides to make arms. The curve softens the squareness of most rooms, rugs, and sofas.

3 **WINGBACK CHAIR:** Fun fact: designed to protect the sitter from drafts, a wingback chair is an armchair with a tall back that angles out at the top. The low arms make it so ergonomic for easy elbow resting and reading.

4 **CLUB CHAIR:** For long game night sessions, this armchair is known to be large, deep, and comfortable. Grab four for a game room, or add a pair across from a sofa for an instant conversation area.

5 **ACCENT CHAIRS:** Here is your opportunity to think a little less about comfort and function and bring in something that adds style to your space. An accent chair can float around or live against the wall next to a credenza, ready for guests.

6 **LOUNGE CHAIR:** Less upright and formal, the lounge chair is designed for hours of comfort— they're deep, ergonomic, and usually call for a footrest or ottoman.

hot tip I've been known to buy "looking at" chairs instead of "sitting on" chairs (like my vintage Paul McCobb). This might seem silly and a waste of space, but looking at them brings me a lot of joy.

7

CHAISE LOUNGE: *Chaise longue* in French literally translates as "long chair," and that's essentially what it is, a long upholstered bench with a back on the shortest side.

be sustainable A vintage chair with good bones can be restored and recovered to become the statement piece your room needs.

BUT WAIT, THERE'S MORE . . .

1 **OTTOMANS, POUFS, AND FOOTSTOOLS**: These pieces aren't always top-of-mind when you're thinking about the furniture you must have, but don't underestimate them, because they're kind of the secret sauce to making your sitting and entertaining spaces as comfortable as they can be. The difference: Ottomans have legs and are more structured; poufs sit on the floor and are more casual.

2 **BENCH**: Think about unconventional uses here. A coffee table when space is limited, perhaps? Or a low sofa table behind a couch stacked with books for visual interest and function? If it's high enough, you could even use it for seating at your dining table.

3 **COFFEE TABLE**: Consider mixing things up with a different shape. If everything in your living room is looking very rectangular (a common problem), a circular or oval coffee table can help break it up! Many a coffee table style also functions as secondhand storage in homes short on space or as a garage for ottomans you don't need every day.

4 **SIDE/END TABLE**: These tables not only are a place to rest your drink but also probably include extra space for lamps, and they are more likely to be a matching pair than an accent table. Some are designed to float, but most have a "back" that's made to sit against the wall. If you're looking for something that does double duty, get one with drawers.

3

5

4

5   **ACCENT TABLE**: Unlike the side table, these tables can go anywhere. They don't typically have drawers, and are smaller and more decorative and versatile than their end table counterparts. Think: mini bar cart, bookcase, or catchall for keys and mail.

be sustainable   If you have the budget to support indie makers and artisans, know that you're also taking part in the next generation of heirloom pieces. Paul McCobb and Milo Baughman were once small makers, and their pieces are now worth a pretty penny, so if you can invest early in a high-quality artisanal piece, you won't regret it.

WHAT'S A "CASEGOOD"?

You'll hear this word around Design Town—what it means is that a piece of furniture has interior storage. Here are a few examples:

CREDENZA: The credenza versus banquette versus buffet versus sideboard argument online is real. For our purposes, the credenza will more likely sit in an office or living room, while the others will typically be seen in a kitchen or dining room. In offices, a credenza is where you keep all the things so that the desk stays clear (or clearer). In living spaces, it is used for storage (think: games, photo albums) and occasionally as a media console, but you may need to drill some holes in the back for cords.

SIDEBOARD AND BUFFET: These two are very similar and could be used interchangeably without most people batting an eye. In general, you wouldn't call something a "buffet" unless it was situated in an eating area. The purpose of this piece of furniture in a dining room is to display or serve food that doesn't fit on the table, and to store serveware or dishes you don't use as often as those in the kitchen cabinets. Traditionally, buffets have longer legs while sideboards have short ones or cabinets that go all the way to the floor. Sideboards have also become well known for being a bit more slender than their buffet counterpart. Their slimmer profile and ample storage also popularized their use in areas of the home beyond the dining room.

HUTCH/CHINA CABINET: Fun fact: Back in the day people didn't have cabinetry. Just a kitchen table and a stove, and storage pieces where they kept everything else. You may think that the difference between a hutch and a china cabinet is one of style or fanciness, and while a china cabinet is reserved for your nicer dishes, the technical difference is that the hutch is technically two pieces—a shelving unit on top of a cabinet—whereas a china cabinet is one continuous piece.

CONSOLE: A console is basically a credenza that stores media equipment. As such, it has holes in the back and sometimes a glass door to help remotes communicate with the devices inside.

BOOKCASES VERSUS BOOKSHELVES: Yes, there is a difference. A bookcase is affixed to a wall more permanently, and is often more custom designed and built into the wall. Book shelves are ready-made and movable (just take out your books and Grandma's urn first). Any custom bookshelf/built-in/ niche should have a minimum of 12 inches of depth for books (15 inches for oversize books). My original built-ins in our hundred-year-old house are too shallow and low to house my collection of heavy coffee table books. Do yourself a favor and give yourself ample depth and height so you don't have to dig out all your novels from college to fill them.

DINING FURNITURE

Other than the couch, any other space where you can sit and eat is usually another huge purchase that is at the forefront of most people's minds when they are buying furniture. Here's how to approach furniture in this room:

CHOOSE YOUR SHAPE

Rectangles and squares are the most classic shape. They clearly delineate where you sit and will fit most rectangular rooms easily. I'm a big fan of oval and round tables, which allow for better flow, especially if you need to walk through your dining room to get to another part of the house. They also give you more flexibility on the number of guests.

CHOOSE YOUR BASE

FOUR LEGS: Like a mammal with a flat back that holds your food. If it gets too long, though, you'll need two supports in the middle, so you'd be looking at six or eight legs.

PEDESTAL: Great for oval and round tables and gives you easy "tuckability" with chairs, since there are no legs to contend with.

TRESTLE: More architectural interest with an old-world feel. Just be sure that you can push your end chairs all the way in, as often the trestle is very wide and blocks the feet from the full tuck.

SAWHORSE BASE: A more industrial look; imagine two saddles supporting a single solid top.

buyer beware
Armless chairs have more flexibility and take up less space, but if you are opting for arms, triple check dimensions to ensure you can tuck them under the table.

CHOOSE YOUR SEATING

CHAIRS: You have the choice of including two armchairs and side chairs. The armchair is also sometimes referred to as the "host," head, or king chair, because these chairs are traditionally positioned at the heads of the table and can even be a different material, style, or size than the side chairs. The side chairs can also be armchairs, but know that you want to shake it up if you can.

BENCH: Many a photo shoot has featured the dining bench, and that's because it looks *good*. However, the dining bench can be a little hard to navigate if more than two adults have to slide in to sit, but it can be a really great way to dress down your dining space, making it feel and look more approachable and eclectic. Benches are also helpful for kids, because they don't have to pull their seats out or in and you can fit so many 'round the table! But if you like hosting long dinner parties, your guests might be bummed about sitting on a bench and may send you their chiropractic bill.

BANQUETTE: The banquette is basically the royalty of the bench. Go for it when you want more space for seating but you want it to be comfy and make an impact visually. Banquettes can be built-ins, or not.

BAR STOOLS VS. COUNTER STOOLS: For most islands you want counter height, not bar height seating. It's a common mistake that you'll know you've made when your friends are trying to cram their thigh meat into six inches of space.

For ultimate comfort and support, choose stools with a supportive back and an upholstered seat. But if the streamlined look is important to you (or if your kitchen backs up to the living room and you want an unobstructed view), skip the backs so your seating tucks fully under the island and blends in with the base.

A built-in banquette is a great place to add hidden storage (drawers or lift-top seats), and a toe kick gives your heels more room when you are sitting up straight.

buyer beware
While there are many performance fabrics on the market, with small kids your best best is vinyl, leather, or an outdoor fabric. And know that they will use pillows as napkins. Kids are monsters like that.

buyer beware A tall bed (like this canopy) needs a tall room or at least an interesting ceiling. If you are bringing the eye up, make sure the trip is worth it at the top.

BEDROOM FURNITURE

The anchor to the bedroom, your bed, not only informs the style of your room, but can also take the room from quiet to dramatic, depending on what frame and style you choose. I'm going to break this down into the four main categories of how I choose a bed, but note: This is less about a specific "style" and more about the impact that it has on the room.

UPHOLSTERED: One word here: *comfort*. Upholstered headboards (and bed frames) give you softness, and you can still add color and pattern in the fabric. The upholstered bed is my personal choice for our bed because, as a nighttime reader, I lean against the headboard a lot and love that I'm guaranteed a pillow effect. Go for a style with special details like pattern or tufting, or keep it simple and neutral and let your bedding pop.

WOOD: Everything from slab, stained, spindle, to painted, wood is a great choice for longevity and adds some structure to your bedroom. I love a classic Shaker spindle bed, which never goes out of style.

IRON: Likely the most classic, an iron bed has a sweetness to it, and there are many modern versions that give the room a more old-world vibe.

CANOPY: If you really want to embrace old-world romance, opt for the four-poster—you feel enclosed in it, almost like a room within your room. There are modern versions out there, or go full-on royalty with dramatic drapes or netting.

THE CLASSIC HEADBOARD

Think of a headboard as a finishing touch to your bedroom design. While they aren't entirely necessary, they can be customized to no end and serve as a great visual statement, adding color, texture, or an interesting silhouette.

But while headboards are about 90 percent aesthetics, there are some things to consider when choosing one beyond style, like how you actually use your bed day to day. If you're a coffee-in-bed type, for instance, an upholstered style will be most comfortable to lean back against. Upholstered headboards need the same lifestyle considerations as sofas and chairs when it comes to fabric choice. Or you might opt for a hardwood or metal headboard stacked with Euro shams for comfort. Just make sure the headboard is high enough so it doesn't get swallowed up in a bedscape of pillows. Another functional consideration: When square footage is lacking, a headboard with built-in storage shelves could be a good alternative to freestanding nightstands. It's hard to DIY furniture, but you can absolutely DIY a headboard, and we have done *many*. It's really about creating a focal point above your bed in a cozy material that complements the other textiles in the room.

ABOVE: Stylist Emily Bowser fully DIY'd this headboard, and, wow, does it completely engage the wall and make it feel super high-end (even though it was on a total budget). If you are into putting in some sweat equity, a homemade headboard will pay dividends.

BOTTOM: Beware of blocking any windows, even with a headboard. Designer Brady Tolbert made this channel-tufted headboard that stretches from wall to wall and serves as a nightstand. Or, skip the headboard, go with a platform bed, and pile on the pillows.

KNOW BEFORE YOU GO

SHOULD YOU BUY A WHOLE BED? Many stores offer the option of just a headboard that you can attach to a standard metal or platform base. While this can be much more affordable and allow for more flexibility, make sure that there isn't a gap between the top of the mattress and the headboard. If your budget allows, go for the complete bed.

DO YOU NEED A FOOTBOARD? Nope. A footboard can make the bed feel more balanced with the headboard, but it's not necessary and can also make the bed look tighter and smaller. It can also be a nuisance for taller people who want to stretch out.

WHAT ABOUT HEIGHTS? Standard bed height is 25 inches from the floor to the top of the mattress to allow you to sit on the bed with your feet on the ground. But many people (myself included) are opting for a lower bed—as low as 18 to 22 inches—to make the bed easier to plop down on.

PANEL VERSUS PLATFORM? The panel bed—a frame plus box spring plus mattress set inside two rails on a base—is being challenged in popularity these days by the simpler platform style, which is just a mattress on a flat surface. Platforms are typically much lower (12 inches to 16 inches), and you don't need a box spring, dust ruffle, or bed skirt. Be sure the bed has a slatted base so the mattress can breathe.

HOW BIG OF A BED? Here are some loose guidelines on how to approach bed shopping.

- Twin: kids and teens. Go for a twin XL, which gives you 5 extra inches of length for taller kiddos.

- Full: With 27 inches per adult, a full is fine for one adult or two adults for a temporary stay.

- Queen: With 30 inches per person, a queen will fit up to two adults and a small pet or two.

- King: With 38 inches per person, the king is king—and great for the whole fam!

be sustainable Buy as if you can't return it. This includes furniture and accessories. Many stores can't resell what you return, especially beds and mattresses (even if their policy lets you return it), so before swiping your credit card ask yourself how sure you are of the purchase. Try it out in stores or read the online reviews very carefully.

BEDROOM STORAGE

Despite the bedroom's almost singular purpose of sleep, one still has stuff, especially if you want to ensure that you leave the house clothed. Sure, it's not the most exciting furniture to think about, but you need good storage. Consider options that don't mess up your sanctuary or clutter your dreams.

In short, bedroom storage furniture runs the gamut, from storage beds to nightstands with drawers, and from storage benches, to armoires, dressers, and tallboys. These are the basics:

NIGHTSTANDS: Fun fact: Originally meant for chamber pots, nightstands have come a long way to create a surface for your water glass, a lamp, books, and any other nighttime necessities. They typically include a drawer and are laid out to flank the bed and are scaled properly to the size and height of the bed. For example, king beds often need wider nightstands to help the room seem balanced.

WARDROBE/ARMOIRE: Want to turn a random room with a window into a bedroom? Add a wardrobe. A rather large, freestanding piece of furniture that has a space for hanging clothes and often interior drawers, these are great for spaces that don't have closets. They'll also make you look fancier than you are (and possibly send you to the hospital after trying to get them up the stairs). This is a great piece to buy vintage or antique, as there are a lot of them on the market that are solid built.

DRESSERS/CHEST OF DRAWERS: We're talking drawers upon drawers—this is where I often splurge on more heirloom pieces. Dressers can be vertical (tallboy, highboy) or horizontal (standard, lowboy). What you choose is mostly determined by what you can fit in your space. A long horizontal one will house the most clothes and be the easiest to access, giving you room above it for a mirror or artwork, but a tallboy can fill that corner space or niche better.

budget tip Vintage or antique armoires are not in high demand and can be found pretty easily and affordably at antique malls.

CINEMA NOW

TEXTILES AND UPHOLSTERY

When you stand back and look at a room, the textiles (rugs, pillows, and throws) and furniture upholstery should feel cohesive, playing off one another to give you the perfectly pulled-together look and feel. But as important as aesthetics can seem, there's more to choosing fabric than what looks good. You don't want to pick upholstery that pills easily on a couch that's going to see a ton of daily use. How a fabric or textile wears, how easy it is to clean, and how expensive it is by the yard (or foot) are major deciding factors.

Much of that decision rests on what the fabric is made out of: natural fibers, artificial fibers, and, most common in this day and age, a combination of the two. Manufacturers will frequently blend fibers together to make them more durable and flexible, and to create different textures and colors. If the thought of choosing between a million and one swatches makes your head spin, take a deep breath and read on for the ones I like to use the most.

THINK BEFORE YOU BUY

It's easy to fall in love with a pattern or a texture, but first consider the following:

WEAR AND TEAR

Where and how often will this fabric be used in the home? Do you have children and/or animals? How cleanable is it? Are we talking spot clean or dry clean only? Or throw-it-in-the-washing-machine-every-two-weeks kind of clean? And what is your personal threshold for said cleaning?

PRICE POINT/YARDAGE

Before you get too attached to that silk faille that is $54 a yard, check with your upholsterer to get an estimate for how much is needed. Keep in mind that fabric can be expensive because of not only the material but also its construction. Sometimes the extra cost is worth it if it means you're going to get ten-plus more years of use.

ALLERGIES

A tighter weave will help keep dust and other allergens from getting through the fabric weave and accumulating under the fibers. Upholstering in a way that is easy to remove and clean is also a good idea, like a slipcover, for example. Obviously, leather and vinyl are easier to wipe down. Low-pile rugs hold fewer dust mites than high-pile ones, and, even better, some newer rugs are made to throw in your at-home washing machine, which could save you hours of vacuuming. (Unless, of course, you find vacuuming to be a form of meditation like some of us.)

HARMONY BETWEEN FABRIC AND FURNITURE STYLE

Unless you're going for an overly eclectic look, you probably don't want to recover your traditional English rolled-arm sofa in purple vinyl. A linen would be a more appropriate choice, given the style of the piece.

pro tip If you don't need a ton of yardage, vintage fabrics (google "deadstock yardage"), hand-dyed throws, quilts, or even thin rugs can all act as upholstery on benches, ottomans, headboards, or pillows.

OPPOSITE: A white chair can be dangerous, but there are a lot of performance fabrics on the market meant to be easily wipeable (see Resources, page 330). Dirt isn't exactly repelled, but they do promise easier cleanup.

be sustainable Buy vintage, thrift, or antique, as much as possible. You don't have to twist my arm. This was my philosophy for years because of financial necessity. It's also the best way to make your house unique. Every room needs something vintage to give it soul—and the good news for you is that this is also good for the planet.

FAVORITE UPHOLSTERY FABRICS

LEATHER: Although leather is technically a hide, not a textile, it's a popular choice for upholstery, so we are adding it in here. Leather can be gently vacuumed, damp wiped, and cleaned with leather conditioner or saddle soap. Since it's sold by the hide, leather upholstered furniture can have some variation in color.

LINEN: With a beautiful, timeless texture, linen gets better with time. It also resists pilling. If you like this fabric, you're likely ready to commit to a lived-in look: It wrinkles and soils easily, and needs to be cleaned professionally, which can be a huge annoyance for anyone with pets, kids, or obsessive cleaning tendencies.

COTTON: Cotton is a popular textile because it is resistant to wear and pilling. Blending cotton with other fibers can strengthen it, making it more family-friendly.

POLYESTER AND MICROFIBER POLYESTER: Like nylon, polyester is rarely used alone and is combined with fabrics to help beef up its durability. When blended with wool, polyester keeps pilling problems at bay. It's also easy to spot clean and great used in spaces that get a lot of sun. Microfiber is even stronger than polyester by itself, which is why it's gotten more popular in recent years.

VELVET: The coziest and softest of all the upholstery fabrics, velvet has come a long way from its original fragility, and when blended with polyester or rayon it can withstand real wear and tear, while still adding a bit glam, texture, and reflection. With a tight weave, velvet is great for those who have cats because they can't sink their claws into the fabric so easily.

pro tip Many fabric labels will tell you whether the fabric is light, medium, or heavyweight, which is a solid clue as to how well it will hold up over time. Lightweight fabrics can give you roughly three years of regular use before you start to see some wear and tear, whereas heavyweight fabrics can handle five times that. Order swatches (where you can also test for spills and spot cleaning) to get a feel for how durable your upholstery is before committing to a bunch of yardage.

While leather is stain resistant, claws can mark it up easily, making it less pet friendly should you have a long-nailed fur baby.

RUGS AND HIDES

Area rugs and hides define spaces and help anchor furniture, both visually and literally. Rugs also create extra coziness underfoot, and bring more (or less!) color and texture to a space.

1 **SHAG:** This long-pile rug is great in a bedroom and cozy living space. And while it hides spills surprisingly well, it may not be best for allergy sufferers, since it can also harbor dust.

2 **CUT PILE:** This style is plush and soft as the "loop" is actually cut to expose the yarn texture. Often with a variety of shades of colored yarns, it can be more forgivable to use.

3 **CUT AND LOOP PILE (TIP-SHEARED):** A combo of loop and cut, with this style you can play with patterns, heights, and even more texture and depth—all in the same rug.

4 **FLATWEAVE:** Woven instead of looped, a flatweave can even be reversible and is typically affordable. There are tons of vintage colorful flatweaves at flea markets that will withstand wear and tear.

5 **PERSIAN STYLE:** The classic Persian rug is no joke, and centuries of skills have gone into weaving these pieces of floor art. From antique to new, these can run a pretty penny but they are so durable, classic, and forgiving. The more well-loved you can find them the better.

6 **ANIMAL HIDE:** For nonsquare areas (like this bay window) a hide can be a flexible floor sculpture. While they are extremely durable and easy to wipe, make sure the one you find has been ethically sourced, and know there are decent synthetic options out there if you like the vibe and shape.

buyer beware Sisal isn't as durable as it looks. Liquids and stains can easily soak in and many people (including my husband) don't love the way they feel underfoot. Try layering them with a softer rug.

7

NATURAL FIBER: If you're on a budget and looking for a large floor covering, check out sisal, jute, hemp, and other grass rugs, which layer well with other styles.

HARD FINISHES AND FLOORING

Choosing materials for surfaces that will become your walls, countertops, and floors is indeed *hard*. These choices are generally permanent and once installed, costly to change out. Plus, there are literally thousands to choose from. We'll cover the top three most commonly used hard finishes: tile, stone, and wood. Then we'll get into more specifics about flooring.

As a general rule and jumping-off point, I like the materials and permanent finishes to reference the architecture and era of the house. That said, there are modern ways to incorporate any style while maintaining the integrity of your home, so you can avoid a look that's super dated. To do it—and to be sure you'll be happy with your decision in the long run—there are two things you'll need to know: some details on your home's architectural style and how you will actually use the home. My motto: Choose what's best for your family, best for the house, and best for the planet. Hopefully that means you choose, buy, and install just once, for the long-term.

TILE | While a white subway tile is always classic (and equally modern), I suggest shopping for tile in person, so you can rule out other styles before making your decision. Here are some of the different tile materials you could be passing up:

1 **CEMENT:** Certainly an exciting choice, given its range of colors and patterns, cement tiles can add a little old-world Mediterranean flair to a room, even when used in modern colors and patterns. They are, however, porous and very easy to stain (even when sealed properly). Install in rooms you like the old-world look (think patios, courtyards, or sunrooms).

2 **ZELLIGE/CERAMIC:** While Zellige tiles, which are handmade in Morroco, used to be a rare find, they are becoming more affordable. Zellige tiles have an organic texture and reflect light beautifully.

hot tip Order at least 20 percent in overage for your tiled surface, both to cover finishing cuts and in case breakage occurs.

3 **PORCELAIN:** Somewhat of a catchall term, porcelain tile, which is made of refined clay and other natural elements, can be made to look like wood, concrete, marble, and so on. The good: They're far less pricey and fragile than the materials they mimic. The bad: Because the pattern or color is printed onto the porcelain, they can vary in quality and look, and yes, some can look really fake and cheap.

4 **NATURAL STONE:** On the more expensive end of the spectrum, natural stone lends an organic feel and warmth to a space. This is a great option for flooring in bathrooms, where it can be difficult to lay stone as a slab, but note that this route is *wildly* more expensive because of the labor involved to cut the stone into tiles. (More on natural stone on page 110.)

TILE FOUR WAYS

A **THE STAGGER**

B **THE STACK**

C **THE HERRINGBONE**

D **THE PARQUE**

MATTE VERSUS GLOSSY

When working on a project, I have spent my fair share of time obsessing over these two tile choices. Matte tile is a bit more modern, but when laid in a staggered pattern, it can still work well in traditional-style homes. Glossy is a good call for reflecting light in darker spaces. I've found both to be equally loveable and easy to clean.

ABOUT GROUT

Somehow, the most boring material ever holds a lot of power in a space. I generally like tile to be the star, but there are times when grout can actually function as a design element. Case in point:

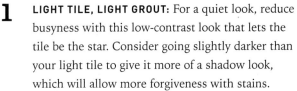

1 **LIGHT TILE, LIGHT GROUT:** For a quiet look, reduce busyness with this low-contrast look that lets the tile be the star. Consider going slightly darker than your light tile to give it more of a shadow look, which will allow more forgiveness with stains.

2 **DARK TILE, DARK GROUT:** With double darkness, you add so much texture and no busyness. This look is seen best when the light hits it. Just go darker with the grout than you think, as it dries lighter and will fade.

3 **LIGHT TILE, DARK GROUT:** This is a look taken literally from the NYC subways. A dark grout highlights the brick shape and creates a pattern on the walls that your eye sees immediately. It's a busier, yet totally classic look.

buyer beware Dark grout can stain some light tiles, so ask about any special installation needs.

4 **DARK TILE, LIGHT GROUT:** Such drama and sexiness. In this look you see the grout first, with the tile receding a bit visually. I love how the grout is picked up in the reflection of this shiny tile, just be sure to seal the white grout so it doesn't stain and it's easier to clean.

STONE SLABS

The sheer size and weight of a stone slab can make choosing this material an intimidating prospect. Add in the long list of care instructions, and slab becomes even more daunting. But there's no denying how beautiful stone can be when cut down and laid into countertops, backsplashes, or entryway flooring. To fast-track your decision making, ask yourself these three questions:

1. WHAT IS YOUR LIFESTYLE?

Think carefully about how you live in your home. Are you an extremely busy person who might not have time to clean up a spill because you'd need to run out the door? Or are you a helicopter parent to your surfaces? Wherever you lie on this spectrum, I promise there is a perfect stone for you.

2. WHERE IS THIS STONE GOING TO GO?

The kitchen countertop? Bathroom vanity counter? Shower floor and surround? As a wall feature? In each of these areas, the stone will be exposed to different kinds of traffic and various levels of moisture. Be aware of the stone's limitations so that you know how to properly care for it.

3. WHAT'S YOUR BUDGET?

Before you set your heart on something specific, set your budget. That includes a realistic minimum you're prepared to spend and a cap on how high you're willing to go. In general, these factors will determine the price of your stone:

THE FORMAT ITSELF: Slabs tend to drive up costs, since they have to be quarried, transported, and shipped from a site. In other words, they're a lot of work. And stone tile is more affordable so if you are doing it on floors or walls it's a good way to save money.

FABRICATION COST: How many cuts are needed, how many seams you'll have, and whether you want it honed or leathered will all factor into the cost. (See page 113.)

INSTALLATION: In most cases, the higher the price of your slab, the higher the installation fee. A fabricator will take measurements, then make a wood template of your project. The fabricator will ensure that the template fits *perfectly* before making any cuts to the stone. This turnaround can take a couple of weeks and can also impact cost, depending on how intricate the installation is.

REAL STONE VS. MAN-MADE QUARTZ

There are two reasons to choose quartz over marble: budget and ease of care. Marble is far more vulnerable to etching and staining (but will chip less) and has a distinct high-end, old-world vibe full of natural veins and organic patterns.

Quartz is more durable, wipeable, and far less porous (meaning it's hard to stain). If you have a classic or vintage home, go for the marble and let it age. But if you have a mid-century or contemporary style home, quartz is a great option.

be sustainable Go the extra mile. While we've gotten in the habit of ordering whatever we want online, make sure that through your purchase, you are promoting a just world. Research where your item or materials come from and who made or sourced them and how, to ensure that your values are in line with the manufacturer or retailer. These days most stores have more visibility and transparency (check their websites).

Your stone fabricator can integrate your sink into the vanity countertop as shown here. This installation features something really organic—the continuing veining— in a simple and streamlined way.

A GUIDE TO CHOOSING STONE

Get a head start on choosing your ideal stone, setting your budget, and knowing what to expect in the upkeep.

STONE	HARDNESS	POROSITY	SEALANT REQUIRED	STAIN RESISTANT	HEAT RESISTANT	SCRATCH
MARBLE, $50–$100/SQ.FT **Recommended uses:** countertops, flooring, wall cladding	**	***	X		X	
GRANITE, $50–$100/SQ.FT. **Recommended uses:** countertops and vanity tops	***	**	X	X	X	X
LIMESTONE, $50/SQ.FT **Recommended uses:** flooring, wall cladding	**	***	X		X	
TRAVERTINE, $40–$100/SQ.FT **Recommended uses:** flooring, wall cladding	**	***	X		X	
SOAPSTONE, $70–$120/SQ.FT. **Recommended uses:** countertops, vanity tops	*	*	X		X	
QUARTZ, $50–$100/SQ.FT. **Recommended uses:** countertops, vanity tops, flooring, wall cladding	**	*		X		X
PORCELAIN, $60–$100/SQ.FT **Recommended uses:** countertops, vanity tops, flooring, wall cladding	***	*		X	X	X

THE PERFECT FINISH

You've chosen the type of stone, now consider it's finish, which from a distance is barely noticeable, but as you'll see below, is important. There are three options—polished, honed, or leathered—and they all have pros and cons. You can get almost any stone in any of these finishes, but if it doesn't already come that way from the stoneyard you will pay a hefty fee to change the finish. Not all stones can be leathered and some are better honed or polished; lean on your vendor for their expertise.

HONED: A more natural-looking finish, honed stone is more matte and lends an organic vibe to a space. Even with sealing, it can stain, but it's harder to see any etching.

LEATHERED: A newer finish, leathering has a matte finish with texture and depth. It hides etching even more that honed stone, but it'll cost you anywhere from $650 to $1,000 more per slab (which may or may not include transportation). Get quotes from your fabricator before you choose this finish if it doesn't come leathered already. Many fabricators aren't able to leather stone, so if this is a look you want, be sure to ask before you even begin working with a fabricator.

POLISHED: The most mainstream style, polished stone is in fact very shiny, which can give it a glam vibe. Polished stone doesn't stain easily, but contact with acidic food or drinks can etch the surface. If, for instance, you set a cut lemon on the surface for an hour, you'll likely have a matte circle forever.

OPPOSITE TOP:
Soapstone needs to be oiled or waxed a couple times a year to protect it and bring out the depth and darkness of the colors, but it's beautiful in its natural state as well. (If not sealed, food splashes can easily mark it for weeks.)

OPPOSITE CENTER:
I opted for an ogee bullnose on the leathered stone in our kitchen, which is a great soft traditional detail that is hard to chip.

OPPOSITE BOTTOM:
Buy or reserve at least 20 percent extra stone if you are going for one that is more rare, because unless you are ordering a standard slab (like Calacutta, Mount Danby, or Carerra), if you come up short you are in trouble.

LEFT: This Zellige tile, installed with a darker grout to create more shadows, works so well to highlight the grays and deeper neutrals in this special powder bath designed by Corbett Tuck.

JUST ADD WOOD

If you want to add warmth in your home, there is no faster way to do it than with wood. While I truly love all woods when applied right, my go-tos are oak, white oak, beech, walnut, and teak for hardwoods, but maple, hickory, cherry, and rosewood have warmer undertones with more dramatic graining, and I love a white English pine or a bleached-out Douglas fir. It's less about the species and more about the finish.

SOFT OR HARD: Hardwood comes from slower growing deciduous trees (that lose leaves in the winter) and are more durable and long lasting (think oak, walnut, beech, rosewood, maple). Soft wood like pine and Douglas fir are more affordable and great as a building material, but can also add so much character in a cabin (especially cabin ceilings).

RECLAIMED OR NEW: All wood is rich with soul, but reclaimed wood—often sourced from falling down barns or 100-year-old structures have real history. While it may have nail holes and other imperfections, we love what that does to a home and that it's a sustainable choice.

be sustainable Like organic food, seek out wood from FSC certified companies to make sure that what you are buying and putting in your home is sourced ethically from responsibly managed forests and that they promote equality in how they harvest.

REAL OR ENGINEERED WOOD FLOORING: Both are real hard wood on the top, but engineered wood is backed with additional structure allowing only limited sanding and refinishing before you strip it too far. There are some incredible companies out there using high-quality, beautiful wood on an engineered structure in a responsible way, giving it more integrity than real wood (see Resources, page 330). Real wood can warp and split with weather, water, and other elements, especially if not acclimated or sealed correctly. But there is a solidness that I love.

CLEAR OR KNOTTY: Want a wood with more consistent graining? Clear wood is the best of the best, with less "defects" like knots or cracks. I personally love a light knotty pine with a matte sealant in a more casual and rustic home, but it can make it busier and has a particular look, especially in large volumes.

MATTE OR GLOSSY: How you seal the wood affects the level of shine you'll get. A matte finish hides far more than a high gloss and feels more modern, less fancy. Many real wood floors take a matte poly or matte Bona finish to simply protect and bring out warmth without adding stain.

STAIN, NATURAL, OR PAINT: Anything can be done (right) but I prefer to bring out the natural grain of the wood rather than try to tweak the color. However, if you are refinishing your flooring and you hate its undertones, now is your chance to tweak it, tone it down, or paint it. While you would never install wood flooring just to paint it, I actually love the look of an old painted floor (just get some expert advice so it doesn't chip constantly).

Instead of painting the stunning wood in their house (as many people do in older Craftsman houses to lighten them up), homeowners Jamie and Craig had restorers bring it back to its natural state. The house is trimmed in Douglas fir, and in keeping with the historical Craftsman style, they used a matte finish.

hot tip Light wood hides dust and hair more than dark wood, which is worth considering if you live with a pet or you hate dusting.

BEYOND WOOD FLOORING

Flooring is the foundation of interior design, which makes it a great place to start when building out a plan for each room. Besides wood, here are other options you might consider.

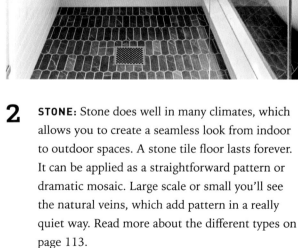

1 **CARPET:** If you want to warm a home in a colder climate, need a soft landing for children, or just like the idea of waking up to a pillow-y cushion underfoot, the good news is that options for wall-to-wall carpets are getting better and better. (Just stay away from anything that looks too cheap in your main living areas.)

2 **STONE:** Stone does well in many climates, which allows you to create a seamless look from indoor to outdoor spaces. A stone tile floor lasts forever. It can be applied as a straightforward pattern or dramatic mosaic. Large scale or small you'll see the natural veins, which add pattern in a really quiet way. Read more about the different types on page 113.

3 **CONCRETE:** With new methods of staining, etching, and polishing, concrete floors, which were typically thought of only for basements, patios, and garages, are now a legitimate option for flooring inside the home. The added bonus is that they may already be there; you just have to remove a layer or two of existing flooring to uncover them. But concrete is very hard and cold and you might find yourself wearing shoes or slippers 24/7.

4 **BRICK:** Calling all farmhouse and cottage lovers. Extremely slip resistant, brick hides dirt very well and is great for mudrooms. You can get creative with the pattern, whether you go with a stagger, stack, herringbone, or parque (see page 106), or another layout you dream up.

ANATOMY OF A STAIRCASE

A **LANDING:** The floor or small platform at the top or bottom of a staircase.

B **RISERS:** They are the vertical pieces that connect the treads.

C **HANDRAIL:** The portion you hold on to that sits on top of the balusters. There are two types: integrated (grooves or ungrooved) or wall mounted.

D **TREADS:** They are the horizontal parts of the steps.

E **NEWEL:** The post at the end, where the railing stops (also my favorite part of the stairs where you can have the most fun).

F **BALUSTRADE:** Aka the railing and vertical pieces (either made of wood or metal) that run from tread to handrail.

G **NOSING:** How the edge of the tread is finished in front. A rounded bullnose nosing is typically found in older homes (and softens falls). Many modern houses have no nosing, stopping at the edge.

H **STRINGER:** The stair-shaped foundation that the treads are adhered to; the actual stair structure (that is often determined by code).

budget tip Applying the balustrades to an iron plate is easier than running each balustrade directly into the floor. I love both looks (and the thinner the balustrade, the more beautiful).

YOU CHOOSE, OPEN OR CLOSED

If building or renovating a staircase, the first question to answer is: Do you want an open or closed staircase? Just how much do you want to see? "Open" means you can see the architecture of each stair from the side; "closed" means that you can't see the stair stringer, and the staircase is usually encased in drywall. This choice will likely be highly informed by the architecture of your home and the visual impact you want your stairs to have in your house.

White paint freshens up a traditional staircase and please note that two wood tones can make it feel more vintage and eclectic.

A hidden stringer like in our home streamlines the entire look, with plaster and metal railing being a classic vintage combination of materials.

Floating open stairs
add a very modern
architectural feature
and feel lighter
than a traditional
staircase.

OPPOSITE: Floor-to-ceiling railings (or pickets) are a great modern way to enclose a staircase while still allowing light through.

ABOVE LEFT: Make a statement with your balustrade pattern. We also love how this balustrade picks up the black of the window frames.

BOTTOM LEFT: Attaching the individual balustrades to the side adds an architectural detail and gives you more real estate for walking (just check your codes to see if this is permitted in your area).

ABOVE: A carpet runner reduces noise and adds a lot of coziness and softness.

CABINETS, MILLWORK, AND PANELING

There are a lot of homes, both old and new, which lack innate character and charm. Maybe these homes are newly built or just need some architectural help, beyond decorative furniture and accessories. But, listen, just because your house was built "basic" doesn't mean it has to stay that way.

Upgrading or rehabbing the cabinetry and adding architectural elements in your home is a good place to put your money. As someone who got their start in this industry focusing on the "stuff" in a room, I will tell you that if you take some time to elevate the architecture of the room itself, then you don't need as many things to make it beautiful.

Enter cabinetry, millwork, and paneling—the beautiful (and often) wooden details in a home.

CABINETS 101

Storage is such a major point of conversation in the design of your kitchen and bathrooms that we had to cover cabinets twice. On pages 220 and 224, you'll find ideas on how to configure these essential units and get a one-of-a-kind look. Here, we're taking a few steps back, to the basics, for a look at how cabinets are constructed and the individual components that go into your overall design.

The more customized your cabinets, the longer they'll take to get installed. On average, lead time for cabinetry is two to three weeks to complete the plans and four to ten weeks to fabricate and install them. Consider this: You won't be able to put in countertops, a backsplash, appliances, or plumbing until the cabinets are installed.

Pricing also goes up as size, material, and the number of details gets more custom. When working with a cabinetry shop, expect quotes anywhere from $15,000 to $80,000.

If those numbers just gave you heart palpitations, ready-made cabinetry kits from IKEA, Home Depot, and other major building supply stores have a lot of off-the-shelf options. The pros of going ready-made: They're more affordable and can look *great*.

But rarely is an older home full of ninety-degree angles, and cabinetmakers, who do custom work, can account for those idiosyncrasies. They'll typically hold off on creating templates or rendering plans until the space is demoed and they can measure down to the millimeter. Custom means perfect; off-the-shelf means there is a larger margin of error in houses both old and new.

hot tip For a cleaner and higher-end look, skip the hardware and opt for concealed hinges, versus the exposed kind, which are visible from the outside of the cabinet.

ANATOMY OF A CABINET

A RAIL: Horizontal pieces or members of a face frame or doorframe, in contrast to a *stile,* which is the vertical member of the frame.

B STILE: Vertical pieces of a face frame or doorframe (in contrast to the *rails,* which are the horizontal members of the frame).

C CARCASS: Sometimes referred to as *carcase,* this is the box or elemental parts that make up the basic structure of a base or wall cabinet.

D TOE KICK: Bottom piece of a base cabinet that is recessed several inches (three inches in depth times four inches in height) from the front surface of the cabinet to allow room for your feet when standing in front of the cabinet. Toe kicks are timeless, but the current trend is to forgo them for a more minimal look.

E FACE FRAME: The wood frame that is attached to the front edges of the top, bottom, and sides of the cabinet box. This frame helps provide rigidity to the box. Cabinet designs that incorporate this feature are called *framed* or *face-frame* cabinets.

F DRAWER FACE: The panel that is attached to the front of a drawer box. It is also referred to as the drawer front and is the visible front part of the drawer where the handle is attached. On some cabinet drawers, the drawer face is the front part of the drawer box.

I'm always a fan of mixing hardware styles—like here with the drawer pulls and the faucet.

CHOOSE YOUR STORAGE

Cabinets add color, style, and storage—so they tend to be a huge focal point and a first priority in mapping out your reno plan, budget, and timeline. Think about them early and often, and consider your lifestyle first.

1 **TRADITIONAL UPPERS AND LOWERS:** These offer the most storage and countertop space, which gives you lots of workspace.

2 **OPEN SHELVING:** Open shelves lend a kitchen an airier feel and are a more affordable option than investing in traditional uppers.

3   **FLOOR-TO-CEILING:** With tons of storage, floor-to-ceiling cabinets maximize extra vertical space, and the room still feels really open.

4   **OPEN BASE:** A set of walnut cabinets or similar custom piece of furniture acts more like shelving than your typical shop cabinets. And, well, it just looks really awesome.

PANEL PERSONALITY

Before you start replacing your cabinets, consider whether they just need a face-lift. Changing the panels will renew your kitchen and save you money. Here are my favorite ways of fronting a cabinet.

1 **SHAKER:** The traditional chameleon of cabinet doors, Shaker style has the recessed flat panel. Depending on the materials surrounding the cabinetry, the look lends itself to many different home styles. You can also mix and match it with flat-panel cabinets. Since Shaker is very popular, there is a wide selection to choose from, typically with a shorter lead time, and they can be budget-friendly. Timeless? For sure.

2 **GLASS FRONT:** Typically used in kitchens on the upper cabinetry to display dishes or more specialty kitchen items, this cabinetry mixes and matches easily with Shaker or flat-panel fronts. With glass, you have an excuse to spice up the back of your cabinetry by adding a design element like beadboard, paint, or wallpaper.

3 **RAW WOOD:** Natural wood tends to have a more casual and warm aesthetic with an industrial vibe. New iterations replace that 1990s maple with lighter wood tones in simpler cabinet profiles.

4 **CHICKEN WIRE GRID:** Swapping out glass or shaker panes for antique chicken coop wire or brass mesh is basically your fast track to farmhouse style.

hot tip Renters (and DIYers), if you don't like your cabinet fronts, see if your landlord will let you remove them and paint all the cabinet surfaces the same fresh color, for instant open shelving.

GET A CUSTOM LOOK FOR LESS

When one of my projects calls for something bold but budget-friendly, here's what I do:

PAINT THE CABINETS A MODERN COLOR. White is a forever classic, but dark kitchens—charcoal and hunter green—are moody, dramatic, and modern, and easy to love for years. The downside? They can make a room feel smaller and darker, and it's not so easy to paint over them with a lighter color if you change your mind down the road.

REPLACE THE CABINET FRONTS WITH MODERN READY-MADE FRONTS. I love going to the online shop semihandmade.com. Simply put, these cabinet fronts and hardware give you a more custom and modern look on an IKEA base (and budget).

OPT FOR OPEN SHELVING. Seriously think about how much closed cabinetry you need. If you aren't heavy on small appliances or storing a ton of pots and pans, an open aesthetic—in the way of shelving rather than cabinets—may be the way to go.

RETROFIT AN ANTIQUE PIECE. You may lose some storage by not taking the cabinet down to the floor, but the one-of-a-kind look of a found hutch might be worth it for the amount of soul it can add to a kitchen.

A sweet patchwork curtain in this cottage covers any mess, allows easy access, and adds so much charm with hardly any cost.

CUSTOM CARPENTRY

Cabinetmakers aren't one-trick ponies. They're often master woodworkers and carpenters whose superpower is turning an awkward corner into a cozy reading nook or an empty wall into a built-in bookshelf. Giving purpose to otherwise underutilized spaces is a nice way to add a little character (especially in boxier, new construction homes) and eke out more storage in smaller rooms. Here are a few of my favorite custom cabinetry projects and some things to keep in mind when mapping out your design for each one.

Many designers would argue that a good set of built-ins is a great investment that will boost your home's resale value—especially if they're quality enough to look original to your home. After all, they're basically furniture you're leaving for the next homeowner after you sell the house.

OPPOSITE RIGHT TOP & BOTTOM: Consider built-ins by the bed and TV, which help keep necessities within reach, but totally out of sight.

OPPOSITE LEFT: A slatted accent wall can help delineate space and create texture, while the bench provides so much storage.

LEFT: Don't forget to integrate lighting into bookshelves before you finalize your design. Picture lights always give built-ins an old-world and high-end feel.

WHEN YOU CAN'T HAVE BUILT-INS

But built-ins are just that—an investment that you may not be ready to take on financially. Until you can save up for the real thing, you have more inexpensive options to tide you over.

BUY IDENTICAL BOOKCASES, especially ones that mimic expensive built-in shelving when placed side by side. Mix freestanding vertical cases with horizontal, wall-hung open cabinets for a really custom look.

PICK A WOOD FINISH THAT COORDINATES WITH YOUR WALLS. Or, if you're feeling especially ambitious, paint your bookcases the same color as your walls.

GO FLOOR-TO-CEILING. Filling every crevice is the trick to convincing someone of your faux built-ins. That includes taking your storage as high as you can vertically. Finish off the top edge of your bookcase with crown molding, and guests will be none the wiser to your cabinet trickery.

INTEGRATE LIGHTING. Some bookcases and shelving come with holes at the back for electronic wires. (If they don't, it's easy enough to drill a few.) These are perfect for running cords for picture lights, sconces, or undercabinet lighting.

ABOVE LEFT: Adjustable shelving allows more room to display wall art and three-dimensional pieces.

LEFT: A custom bench was "dad DIY'd" to curve around the corner, expanding the living room in such a smart way.

hot tip Consider using molding to create a line as a stop point when installing wallpaper to avoid overwhelming the room with the same pattern from floor to ceiling.

DEFINING MILLWORK

A **CASING:** The trim around doors and windows.

B **CROWN MOLDING:** Running along the top of the wall or cabinet, along the ceiling, crown molding was traditionally used to hide imperfections. Today, it's more about adding charm, though I'm sure it's probably still used to hide things.

C **CHAIR RAIL:** An applied molding strip that sits roughly 32 inches up from the floor.

D **PANEL MOLDING:** Refers to any type of wall treatment that runs a portion of the length of the wall, typically along the line of a traditional chair rail (see above). While some people think wainscoting involves only beadboard or V-groove, the "halfway method" can be used for any type of paneling.

E **BASE MOLDING:** Sort of the opposite of crown molding, this molding is where the floor meets the wall. It can be finished with shoe molding, which is also called quarter round and is a narrow strip that hides gaps between the base molding and the floor.

budget tip If you want to DIY applied molding, don't splurge on expensive wood—get primed paint grade versus stained grade to save money since you know you are going to paint the wood.

E

MORE MILLWORK

Using carpentry, or specifically millwork, to create a decorative or classic look is where we'll focus our attention from here on out. Traditional home? This section is a toy for your toy box! But even modern homes can have fun with woodwork.

1 **WAINSCOT** is any wood paneling that is on the bottom half of the room. This can be V-groove, beadboard, or shiplap. It's usually finished with a decorative trim, but feel free to keep it simple.

2 **BOX MOLDING** consists of strips of wood that are either glued or nailed in a box pattern and then painted in the same color as the wall. You can customize not only the size of the boxes—think squares, rectangles, or a combo of each—but also the thickness of the strips to achieve just about any look.

3 **BOARD AND BATTEN** typically consists of a wide "board" and then a smaller, narrower "batten," which is installed over each of the seams, creating a stronger and more energy-efficient structure. When used on interior walls you don't need to have the larger board; you can instead fake the look with small strips installed vertically.

4 **V-GROOVE PANELING,** which falls under the vertical paneling family, is a type where the edges of the boards have been shaved so that when they butt up against one another, each groove forms a V shape. It's traditional with a twist, and it can go either vertical or horizontal.

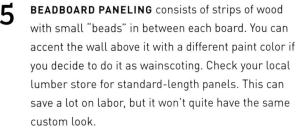

5   **BEADBOARD PANELING** consists of strips of wood with small "beads" in between each board. You can accent the wall above it with a different paint color if you decide to do it as wainscoting. Check your local lumber store for standard-length panels. This can save a lot on labor, but it won't quite have the same custom look.

6   **VERTICAL PANELING** might evoke 1970s basements covered in shiny fake wood. But when done the modern way, vertical paneling can bring a ton of character and texture to a room. The trick is customizing the size of the plank to create a drastically different look from the vintage style and even painting it in a bold color.

7

HORIZONTAL PANELING takes the vertical paneling concept and turns it on its side. But it's not to be confused with shiplap. While **SHIPLAP** is a *type* of horizontal paneling, it traditionally has a space in between the boards (which are designed to easily fit together), whereas horizontal paneling (like vertical) can be installed butt to butt without a space, depending on the look you are going for.

I love mixing up the orientation of the paneling as shown here with horizontal paneling and a touch of vertical to help frame the window.

THE FIREPLACE

If I were running for president of Good Ambience, I would run enthusiastically on a "pro-fireplace" platform, heralding the transformative power that flames can add to the mood and, yes, warmth of a room.

The two most common types of fireplace are wood and gas, and there is a pretty stark difference between the two on the ease scale. Before you decide, ask yourself a couple questions: Do you value romance and don't mind working for your ambiance? In that case, wood-burning might be for you.

How often do you want to enjoy a fire? Every night? Then have a remote-controlled gas fireplace installed and invest in pretty porcelain logs and natural stones (over those bright neon rocks that look so fake). In either case, be sure to get your chimney inspected annually.

The fireplace is also where you can inject a lot of style, as it's a natural statement and focal point. I had to design six different fireplaces in one year after never designing one before, so I took a deep dive into fireplaces and learned a *lot*. Let's take a closer look at some great examples.

WHAT FUELS YOUR FIRE

WOOD BURNING

Look forward to crackling sounds, woodsy smells, and so much physical and emotional warmth. It's a lot of work and maintenance and requires an annual inspection by a professional. You have to buy and split the logs, store them in a dry place, light the fire each time, clean the firebox, and maintain the chimney. Some smoke might also come into the house, and the saddest news of all is that, yes, depending on what is in the wood you are burning, you could be breathing in something that might be unhealthy.

GAS BURNING

Want a fire at the switch of a button or turn of a key? Then go for a gas-burning fire. Natural gas is oddly inexpensive, although it is a fossil fuel and prices fluctuate. Gas is more expensive up front to install: You'll need to hire a plumber and invest in connecting the gas line to your fireplace, the cost being directly proportional to how far away the fireplace is from the gas line. Opt for the more natural-looking logs—you still aren't fooling people, but the bright neon rocks can feel jarringly fake. If you go the gas route, consider installing direct vent gas inserts, which keep the heat inside the house.

ELECTRIC

Electric fireplaces mostly have a two-dimensional flame, and are all about the ambience. They can be more environmentally-friendly than gas or wood, and the technology is getting better every year.

hot tip If you have natural gas but your heart is pining for real wood, talk to your fireplace technician about converting to wood-burning but keeping the gas line as a log lighter. You get the smell and crackle of real wood with the ease of a gas flame to start the fire (no Boy Scout skills required).

be sustainable Wood and gas both emit fumes into our environment, so be mindful of how often you use your fireplace (and don't just throw on a few logs and leave the room).

ELEMENTS OF A **FIREPLACE**

You can go traditional with more decorative elements or minimalist, but your fireplace will almost always consist of these elements.

A **MANTEL AND LEGS:** The "legs" and mantel can be wood if they are a safe distance from the firebox, but check local codes.

B **SURROUND:** Typically, your surround consists of fire resistant and noncombustible stone, tile, or metal.

C **FIREBOX:** The area where you build your fires, which protects the fireplace from high temps and flames. They can be made of masonry or come prefabricated.

D **HEARTH:** The flooring in front of a fireplace that extends out into your room. It's a great decorative moment, but should be made of something noncombustible, like brick or stone, to protect your floors and home from stray embers, sparks, and scorching logs that may roll out of the fireplace.

OPPOSITE: Mixing two stones—one as surround, the other as the "legs and mantel"—is a simple way to add a custom look.

ABOVE: Using a simple staggered brick pattern, with slate tile for the hearth, our photographer Sara Tramp integrated a clean, classic look into her traditional Craftsman.

Want a TV above your fireplace? Plan for it. I only do this when it's the Samsung Frame TV, which displays digital art when it's off, and sits flat against the wall.

FIREPLACE STYLES

If you have the luxury of replacing or adding a fireplace, consider the following types.

1 TRADITIONAL/MASONRY: For this style, the fireplace and chimney are built on-site and made out of stone or brick and mortar. You can have a mantel or not, but regardless, this setup is part of the home's structural design and, with proper maintenance, will typically last decades longer than a factory-built fireplace. This is very typical of traditional-style homes or midcentury homes; less so for contemporary.

2 PREFABRICATED/FACTORY BUILT: Fireplace technology and design have come a long way, and now there are many options in finish and style. Think freestanding, inserted into a flat drywall, or even hanging from the ceiling. These are designed, sent, and installed as one cohesive unit, rather than built on-site. Instead of a brick chimney, a round metal chimney is common, and you have options in what the firebox looks like.

3

STOVE STYLE: Gaining popularity *again* (did it ever go away?), this sweet style is prefabricated (or antique) and harkens back to the more utilitarian function of warming fingers and toes in the cabin. For homes that don't have an original chimney (or one in good shape) or a gas line, woodstoves are relatively easy to have installed with a new vertical chimney pipe that exits your home and extends above your roof (though the pipe can typically be shorter for gas stoves).

be sustainable Opt for direct vent or stoves that have the flame enclosed, otherwise it just sucks the air from the room up through the chimney, essentially removing heat and increasing your heating bill, while still producing a flame.

ALL THE AMBIANCE

Non-working fireplace? No problem! Put those updater skills to work and make it a focal point of your room.

Here are a few ideas to get you started:

PAINT THE SURROUND. Take a risk and paint the surrounding bricks and woodwork something dramatic to contrast with the rest of your room.

FILL IT WITH CANDLES. Seek out a variety of tall and short candles, then stagger them in the firebox. I promise you won't even miss the crackle once you turn the lights down low and light them all!

STYLE THE MANTEL. The mantel is another great surface for leaning art against the wall and showcasing your "smalls." Keep the collection rotating so you never get bored.

hot tip A gas insert installed in a traditional firebox is an eco-friendly and efficient way to heat your home by fireplace.

WALL FINISHES

As much as I wish it were, the simple question *What color paint should we choose?* is hardly the only one to ask yourself when it comes to livening up your walls.

First, you'll need to learn your level—understand the texture that you want on your walls beneath the paint. If you love that flat finish look—aka a "smooth coat"—then get ready to pay. The smoother you want your walls, the more labor it takes, which is why most builder-grade walls have a spray texture coat.

Then it's time to think about paint. In addition to color, the finish of the paint you choose can have as big an impact on the style of your room as do your furniture and decor. Then again, maybe you don't want to paint at all but are in the market for some wallpaper. Where do you start with all the options for dressing up your walls? First, let's peel back the layers.

PAINT, COLOR, SHEEN, OH MY

How do you choose the perfect color? I truly wish there were a science to it. But testing the paint in your space on multiple walls and looking at the samples at different times of day is really the only way to achieve what feels right to you. As you apply more coats and as the sun shifts, the color will change and you'll pick up on tones you may or may not love.

Here is some guidance on choosing the finish. All paint companies have their own measure of sheen, so check with their site or a rep to confirm how their specific finishes are defined.

FLAT: Fully matte, with no reflection whatsoever. We love this look because it's so clean and fresh, but it marks up easiest, and retouching can be very obvious. With that in mind, it's best for bedrooms or low-traffic areas.

EGGSHELL OR SATIN: Our favorite of the finishes because it isn't shiny but it's more durable and forgiving than a flat finish. Great for living areas, kitchen walls, and bedrooms.

SEMIGLOSS: As the name implies, there's a little sheen here, and with it a greater barrier against scuffing and chips. Good for moldings, baseboards, bathrooms, or any space that tends to get scuffed or will need to be wiped off easily.

HIGH-GLOSS: More for decorative drama, high-gloss is just that—super shiny and reflective. I've never used it on walls, but some people do, to really bounce the light around and create a dramatic mood. Be sure you have a smooth wall finish to start with, as high-gloss will show every imperfection.

LACQUER: Historically, the word *lacquer* meant super shiny and durable, but there are different sheen levels of this extradurable spray paint. A lot of cabinetry is painted in lacquer to reduce the number of chips and dings. High-gloss is intense, dramatic, and, well, *intense*. This is not a DIY job; be sure to hire skilled painters to achieve the perfect finish.

hot tip You aren't bound to the paint swatch. If you love a color but wish it were, say, 30 percent lighter, you can have that color mixed. Designers do this all the time to get the exact shade they want.

TAKE IT NEXT-LEVEL

If you're looking for a little character beyond a "new construction" look, that's where a finish comes in. There is a wide range—some options are weirder than others—but I'd put my money on these more common options.

1 **ORANGE PEEL:** This is a texture spray that requires a bit of prep to apply it and has the subtle bumpiness of an orange peel when painted over. This application is fast and inexpensive, but it can look dated, especially with semi- or high-gloss paint finishes. Use it to save money in rooms that may be less important to you (finished basements and laundry rooms, for example).

2 **LIME WASH:** This is a chalky finish made of crushed limestone and water that looks a little like suede when applied. It's an eco-friendly and hypoallergenic option that is a great alternative to the pricier plaster look. Beware that the color can be unpredictable, since it's ten times darker when wet and can dry at varying shades, depending on the surface beneath.

3 **BASIC PLASTER:** A warm, hand-done texture that looks great in older homes, though you may need to match the existing plaster in some spots. I would skip it in the bathrooms, however. We recommend a flat paint or, even better, a lime wash there. Notice that the handiwork involved for basic plaster is expensive because it's done with a trowel and applied fairly evenly.

4 **VENETIAN PLASTER:** Sometimes known as lime plaster, Venetian plaster is mixed with marble dust, layered on with a trowel, and then burnished until smooth. The end result: a durable, marble-like surface. It's easy enough to DIY, but what you save on labor, you'll want to use for buying a high-quality product. The difference is between a really thick paint and a true plaster composed of acrylic and marble dust.

5

HEAVY PLASTER: On the most textured (and expensive) end of the spectrum, these hand-troweled finishes can lend a heavy dose of depth to ultramodern, clean-lined spaces. This is a nice way to make a "too perfect" space feel a little lived-in, but it's not great for high-traffic areas that are prone to moisture.

budget tip To hide inconsistencies in the dry wall created by screws and joint compound, try a light hand texture, rather than a sprayed texture. It's more cost effective than plaster (though a bit more expensive than sprayed texture), but will add nice warmth to a space.

Sara Ruffin Costello used the same color on the moldings as on the walls, only in a semi-gloss finish, which reflects the light and creates a subtle texture contrast.

WALL TO WALLPAPER

Done correctly, wallpaper really *makes* a room. Not only does it provide a big dose of pattern and an instantly more "finished" look, but it also actually eases your work on the rest of the room design, guiding your selection of complementary patterns, color, and motifs. Read on for more info on how to narrow your options.

1 CHOOSE THE TYPE

Find the wallpaper that's right for your walls.

NONPASTED. The paper roll doesn't come with any adhesive on it, which can make for a messy installation process. However, nonpasted wallpapers tend to have the longest-lasting results.

PREPASTED. Just add water to the back of the wallpaper and the glue on this type of paper is ready to go. But "activating" the adhesive also means it could more easily peel away from your walls.

SELF-ADHESIVE. Also known as peel-and-stick or temporary wallpaper, this is like a giant sticker that requires a lot of time and patience to install well. It's a great option if you're living in a rental or if you like to redecorate often.

2 DECIDE ON THE MATERIAL

Wallpaper is made of more than just paper. Here are some popular options:

VINYL. Most commonly used and typically prepasted, vinyl is easy to hang and remove. I find it looks better in a more contemporary space than in a traditional one. Some vinyl papers are even washable and moisture resistant, a great option for bathrooms or damp areas.

PAPER. The classic choice, though a very delicate one. Take extra care when handling it to avoid tears and scratches.

FABRIC. The upper echelon (read: the best) of the wallpaper materials, fabric papers don't come prepasted and can be very difficult to hang, so hire a professional to ensure all those bubbles get smoothed out.

GRASS CLOTH. Made from natural fibers, including grass cloth, hemp, jute, reed, or arrowroot, these wallpapers don't require matching, which makes them easier to hang.

3 PICK THE PATTERN

There are so many different patterns to choose from when it comes to wallpaper, but if you are planning to hang the wallpaper yourself, consider these options, which should be noted on the wallpaper roll label.

RANDOM MATCH. This style doesn't require the pattern to be perfectly lined up, which is ideal for a beginner installer.

STRAIGHT MATCH. The pattern here is going to line up vertically, requiring a bit more skill to hang.

DROP MATCH. This style typically features the most intricate designs and means that you will have to line up the pattern both vertically and horizontally. Although it is the most difficult (in other words, hire someone else to do it), the results are the most impressive.

4 SIZE IT RIGHT

Be sure to measure twice when buying your own wallpaper. Multiply the height and width of your walls to get the square footage. Our trusted wallpaper installer suggests always adding four to six inches to the height of your walls, which gives you a bit more flexibility when lining up the paper and then cutting off the excess.

Most companies will let you know the number of square feet that each roll covers. But the square footage only matters so much. It's the size of the pattern repeat that dictates how much paper you need. A bigger pattern equals a larger repeat equals more paper needed. Lean on the manufacturer to help you get the right quantity and opt for thirty percent overage.

One more thing to keep in mind: Wallpaper is made in batches. To ensure your paper matches exactly, buy extra from the start and double-check that the labels all list the same batch number.

ABOVE LEFT: You might think a gold and white pattern would be glam, but it can be a lot quieter than you'd think. The light reflects around it in a really pretty way, adding a lot of life.

LEFT: I LOVE a bold wallpaper in a closet. It's a quiet luxury in an oft-neglected space that brings a lot of smiles while you're dressing.

ABOVE: Wallpaper in a bathroom? Yes. Just keep it away from water sources and use a fan when showering to reduce steam (it's best in a powder bath).

LIGHTING, APPLIANCES, AND PLUMBING

Whether you're renovating or updating, at some point you may have to open up those walls to make your home a little smarter and brighter. Luckily, wireless technology has reduced our need to add wired-in luxuries like sweet sound systems (though many new builders are still adding those in). But even installing a new convenient outlet or a set of pretty sconces needs to be carefully considered, especially in older homes.

You might be at the point in the construction phase of a renovation where you have opened up walls. Before you can get into the fun part of choosing between pendants and chandeliers, you need to have an official electrical plan in place. While your intentions at the beginning of your project may not have been to totally redo your electrical, this is your chance to make your home more efficient, and to add changes that can enhance each room's ambience and, quite possibly, your quality of life.

WHAT IS AN ELECTRICAL PLAN?

1 **WALK THROUGH YOUR HOME AND IMAGINE WHERE LIGHT SWITCHES AND OUTLETS SHOULD GO.** This should be intuitive. When you walk through the front door, there should be an entry light switch, as well as one for exterior lights. If a wall is going to be blocked by furniture or an eventual custom cabinet, consider where those outlets might go instead. (Stay aware of places electrical wiring cannot go, such as inside pocket door walls.) And as a rule of thumb, outlets are typically placed every six feet, but check local codes, particularly for bathrooms and kitchens, as this may vary.

2 **DETERMINE WHERE THE J-BOXES WILL BE PLACED.** This can dictate your options for certain styles of lighting fixtures. If you don't already have your lighting picked out, have your electrician leave a "loop" of extra wiring so they can easily move the junction box down or up (and thus change the location of the light) without opening up the entire wall.

3 **PLACE YOUR OUTLETS BASED ON YOUR DREAM LIFESTYLE.** This is your chance to have them in your floor to plug in lamps (if you have a basement or crawl space) and right behind nightstands. Think about where your TVs might be hung or placed to ensure the proper outlets will sit behind them. And here's where you can add double outlets (called gangs) for your hair dryer, and USB outlets in your kitchen island.

4 **FINALIZE YOUR PLAN.** And then finalize it again. Be sure to do a full walk-through with your electrician to make sure you both know the lighting plan and where those lights connect to. To save you stress later, once everything is installed but before you close up the walls, take a photo of your electrical, and plumbing, and even jot down exact measurements for each location.

5 **START SHOPPING** for lighting and appliances!

MISSED OPPORTUNITIES

OUTLETS IN THE MIDDLE OF THE FLOOR: Here's a controversial hack. By making a tiny slit in the rug, your cord can thread right through.

ISLANDS AND PENINSULAS: An outlet plus power strip combo placed inside drawers and cabinets make for an instant charging station for phones, small electronics, and appliances.

DIMMER SWITCHES: Adding a few dimmers here and there can change the way the space feels just with the click of a switch (plus, it's an easy DIY). Just know that when you pair LED lightbulbs and dimmers they can flicker when you turn them on, so look for LED-compatible dimmer switches.

REPLACING OUTDATED SCONCES: Just be sure you know the width of the J-box hole so that you can buy a fixture with a canopy that fully covers the old hole. And if not, you can use a larger wooden medallion—paint it the same color of your wall—to hide the excess space.

NEWER, SMARTER OUTLETS: Swap out old, loose outlets for smarter ones—GFCI plugs for kitchens and baths, and USB options near the bedside and sofa for your phone.

USB CHARGING OUTLETS: Have them near nightstands so you can enjoy a lamp and also charge your devices (should you want them near you at night).

AN APPLIANCE GARAGE: Have a place to store your toaster, blender, coffee maker or kettle. Make sure you have enough outlets for all of them, if you use them daily. Think about outlets inside your medicine cabinet if you want to charge your toothbrush or shaver inside the cabinet.

NICER LOOKING OUTLETS AND SWITCHES: Splurge on these in places of prominence in your main areas—where you see them constantly. It's an upgrade that feels a little superfluous, but it's a daily joy, both visually and functionally, when you interact with them.

ABOVE: I love when lighting feels like it's in the same family—they don't need to be twins, but cousins like this sconce and semi-flush-mount in the kitchen.

OPPOSITE TOP LEFT: You don't have to have professional wiring or call an electrician to have a nice looking bedside sconce. This plug-in is so chic (and the cord disappears on the black wall).

OPPOSITE TOP RIGHT: A brass-plated knob light switch brings so much vintage charm, with modern function.

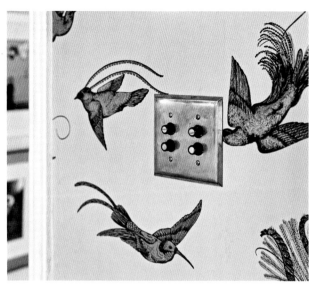

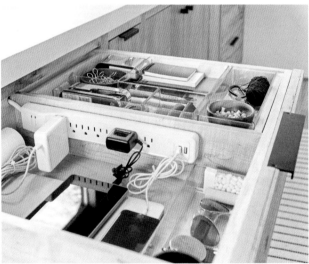

BOTTOM LEFT: Our junk drawer houses a charging station for phones and tablets, keeping the counters clear and temptation at bay.

BOTTOM RIGHT: We splurged on black metal outlets for our black island to make them disappear (look for outlet options to match your cabinet color, or paint them a custom hue).

LIGHTING

As a big-time romantic, I think that lighting plays a huge part in ambience, which really affects your mood when you are in a space.

A well-lit room should include three different types of light that every room needs:

AMBIENT

This is where a room's overall illumination comes from, typically natural light from your windows and the lighting that substitutes for natural light in the form of ceiling fixtures or lamps with fabric shades.

ACCENT

These are your more decorative fixtures that work to shine a light on your decor, artwork, or the architectural features of a room.

TASK

As the name implies, these fixtures provide the illumination you need to perform tasks like cooking, reading, or applying makeup in a bathroom.

rule breaker (top right) Erica Reitman hung a huge vintage chandelier practically at the ceiling, adding so much drama which brings your eye up (as well as producing so much light).

RIGHT: A vintage plug-in task lamp hung on a wall adds a cool architectural feature in our otherwise blank basement.

I love how this sconce and the painting work together to create one focal point—it's like a picture light, but less expected.

LIGHTS TO LOVE

Considering each light separately, and with regard to the individual decor "zones" of a room, will create much more visual interest than throwing up a single, "bright enough" ceiling mount.

1 **RECESSED:** Formerly known as *canned* lighting, these used to be big and bulbous, but modern recessed lighting can be much smaller, square, and even black or wood (just expect to spend a lot more). Don't blow your budget here, but if this is your main overhead element, you are going to want to make your eyes happy when they look at it.

2 **TRACK LIGHTING:** For those just updating, track lighting can be really useful. It's great to be able to direct the lights where you need them.

budget tip Consider a spotlight in place of a track for overhead task lighting. Just make sure that the spread of the light is wide enough for your needs.

3 **FLUSH OR SEMIFLUSH:** In addition to or instead of recessed lights, these fixtures are generally placed in the middle of a room. For multiple lights, they are usually evenly placed. They add a decorative element, and for a lot of older homes, these are the only lighting a room has. If they have enough wattage, that is totally fine. Get rid of those ubiquitous, cheap "boob lights," the flush-mount lights with a finial in the center.

4 **CHANDELIERS AND PENDANTS:** These not only add a huge decorative element, but they can also provide additional task or ambient light for your nights of puzzling. Fun fact: Typically chandeliers have multiple lights and pendants only one.

5 **SCONCES:** Choosing whether you have a single, double, or more architectural sconce is determined by how much light you need and how much wall space you want to dedicate to the sconce.

Renters, look for plug-in options and think about installing conduit to cover the cord that runs along the wall (bonus points if you paint the conduit the same color as your wall).

6 **TABLE AND FLOOR LAMPS:** Enough with the J-boxes and planning ahead. Table lamps are plug and play: Buy multiples, rearrange, and repeat.

be sustainable Save the planet and your energy bill with warm and beautiful lighting you can get with new LED bulbs.

HEIGHT AND SCALE

While the height of a fixture you'll need depends on the fixture itself and on the height and size of the room, and can even vary by room, here are some overall suggestions for hanging fixtures so your pro-basketball player brother doesn't concuss himself on your vintage Murano glass chandy.

- Unless installed over a dining table or bed, light fixtures should hang at least seven feet from the ground—and higher if you have extra-high ceilings.

- When placing your sconces, note where the light source is on the fixture. Does it swing up on an arm, or down? Is it on the top or the bottom? I usually like the wall light source to sit around six feet high, unless you have an architectural feature to account for or higher ceilings.

- If you are repeating the same sconce in the same room, they should all be at the same height, unless there is an architectural feature in the way.

APPLIANCES

Forget what you learned in preschool; in the home design world, *A* is for *appliance*. There are thousands of machines designed to help you prep, cook, and preserve food, but for the purposes of today's lesson, we're going to focus on the essential large-format appliances that every kitchen needs.

If you fancy yourself a cook at all, you most likely know not just the basic tools of the trade required to put a meal together, but also the different configurations, heat sources, and maybe even a few bells and whistles to make cooking easy and—I'm just gonna say it—enjoyable.

Stainless appliances ruled supreme for decades as the braggable higher-end choice. But now you have way more options in color, different metallics, and even the option of hiding completely with cabinetry for the most seamless look.

Velinda Hellen created the perfect work triangle for her clients' kitchen. With the matching stainless steel appliances, the room feels very pulled together (but you don't have to match the appliances—we love a statement range).

COOKING APPLIANCES

Cooking appliances come in all kinds of configurations. Before you shop, consider your kitchen triangle and what might be the most efficient set-up.

1 COOKTOPS sit on top of your counter and have only burners, no oven. This is great if you want a double oven and don't want to put a bulky range in front of a window. There is a downdraft (page 192) that can pop up, though the mechanism will eat up some of the cabinet space you're gaining.

2 RANGES include a cooktop with a built-in oven. These can include features such as a warming drawer, broiler, griddle, and a double oven.

be sustainable Induction ranges not only keep your interior air cleaner, but also don't burn any fossil fuel unlike gas ranges. If you are on the fence, lean induction (I did).

3   **WALL OVENS** are separate units from the cooktop or range and can be ordered as either a single or a double oven—a nice option if you are one who bakes often and have the wall space to spare.

4   **MICROWAVES** now come with fancy cooking features, but think twice before mounting one high above the cooking range; for easy access, you'll want to install it at or below eye level. Be sure to double-check the clearances needed for adequate ventilation. Many people are opting for a **SPEED OVEN** that acts as an additional oven as well as a microwave.

VENTILATION

The ventilation you need depends on how powerful your range is and the sort of cooking you do. Beyond that, it's a matter of style and kitchen layout, as well as the scope of your kitchen makeover.

1 UNDER-CABINET: This simple hood is intended to be installed inside a cabinet or custom framing, making it super easy to camouflage.

2 DOWNDRAFT: A vent that clears smoke and odors from below the appliance, a downdraft is great for an area where you don't want to block the view, such as near a window.

3 **CEILING MOUNTED:** Installed from the ceiling, these hoods can go anywhere in the kitchen (even over islands).

4 **HOOD INSERT:** Installed in a custom cabinet, this style camouflages your ventilation completely, helping you get the most seamless look with your cabinetry.

hot tip The hood's "capture area" should be 6 or more inches wider than your cooktop. The underside should sit 30 to 36 inches above the range—though you can get away with 24 inches for electric ranges.

REFRIGERATORS

Your refrigeration needs all depend on the amount of people in your household and how often you cook. Having a huge fridge that swallows up produce to the point that it rots does no one any favors. The style and door configuration is all a personal preference, and I definitely recommend going to a showroom and testing out all of them. As a huge home cook, I love a dedicated fridge and freezer column, which maximizes the space for both, but when I was an apartment dweller in my twenties in New York I could have had a minifridge or a Smeg and been fine.

A splurge for sure, but oenophiles love wine fridges. They can often be set to two different temperatures—one for red and one for white. Cheers, I'll be over in five.

YOUR CHOICE: HIDE OR SHOW OFF

Choosing the right appliances for your cooking needs is a major undertaking in itself; but figuring out how to show them off in beautiful action is another. Some people love having others see their appliances, others not so much.

Your choices, then, are to expose or to integrate your appliances.

In general, integrated appliances are a design choice you'll have to make early in your kitchen renovation journey. Having those specs laid out before the cabinets are built is critical, because those cabinets will be constructed at a different depth and width than the rest of your cabinetry to accommodate the lack of doors. And even though it's a more luxury choice, integration is not just for big kitchens. It's a great option in a smaller space, where a seamless run of cabinetry can reduce visual clutter.

One thing to keep in mind: If you enclose your wall oven, you will need to install retractable doors, as the oven can't heat up (or cool down) while doors are closed. Make sure your contractor knows what your preference is early on so he doesn't build it without the space for proper hinges.

If you can't integrate your cooking appliances, then consider the newer slide-in ranges. You'll get that built-in look. But note that if replacing an existing range, you'll likely have to replace the backsplash behind it. It's a good opportunity to add tile or another wipeable surface that will be subject to splashy oils and sauces.

hot tip Integration is not just for big kitchens! It's a great option in a smaller space, where a seamless run of cabinetry can reduce visual clutter.

PLUMBING

You know the saying "It's what's on the inside that counts"? Well, there are no truer words when it comes to plumbing your kitchen and bath. The most important, not to mention expensive, part of a bathroom reno is installing the pipes behind the walls. Your faucet is just the cherry on top. Keep in mind:

DON'T WAIT. While choosing faucets seems like something you can put off, get ahead of that decision. Whether you want a deck-mount or wall-mount faucet, an undermount or claw-foot tub—such decisions can affect installations and even permits. And that can create a domino effect, which can hold up your project. Have the plan in place and the valves and fixtures ordered before rough plumbing begins.

PLAN IT OUT and know the date of your "rough plumbing," which is when all the pipes get well mapped out, holes drilled through walls, and studs and everything in its place ready for the final fixtures. You do the rough plumbing when the walls are opened up.

ORDER ALL THE PARTS (and make sure they work together). It's not just a faucet. The valves are the part of the fixtures that go behind the walls and you need the valves during the rough-in phase, but they are usually sold separate from the faucet. If you are placing the orders have your GC double-check to make sure you aren't missing anything and there aren't any red flags with your order.

CHECK YOUR CODES. Each state has different water flow codes and regulation. Want body sprays in your spa shower? Make sure you can actually use them while your overhead shower is on because in some states you can't.

THE KITCHEN SINK

Your sink is like the filling station of your kitchen in many ways, fueling your cooking, your cleaning, and the many everyday tasks in between. Aesthetically, it's often a cornerstone of your design. Let's consider a few options.

1 **TOP MOUNT:** This is a drop-in sink with a lip or rim around the basin that sits on top of the counter. They're easy to install and can be composed of any material, but cleaning gets tricky, as debris collects where the lip of the sink and the counter meet.

2 **UNDERMOUNT:** Installed directly under the sink, undermounts give you a seamless look. However, the material must be lightweight (cast iron and fireclay won't typically work), since they are installed by gluing the basin to the underside of your countertop.

3 **FARMHOUSE:** Also known as an apron sink, which extends beyond the edge of your countertop. Seen mainly in traditional- or farmhouse-style homes, they tend to take up a lot of counter space, so they are ideal in kitchens that have a little extra counterspace for other cooking needs.

FAUCETS

When choosing the finish of your faucet—be it brass, nickel, chrome, black, or copper and a matte, polished, or living finish—consider the other metals that will also be incorporated into the design of your kitchen, such as appliances and cabinet hardware. Either keep it consistent with a single finish or really mix and match them evenly throughout the space.

A **WALL-MOUNTED:** These are ideal for smaller areas where you need to save counter space and maximize your sink's surface area. There are lots of options out there to choose from in an array of styles and finishes. Be sure to calculate height accordingly, to minimize splashing. And leave the installation work to an experienced plumber, since the valves will be enclosed behind the wall.

B **DECK MOUNT:** These sit on your counter and holes are drilled into your countertop beforehand. Know your spread (8 inches on center, for instance) and amount of holes (1, 2, or 3). Even if you have a wall-mounted faucet and handles, you'll likely need to deck-mount the spray nozzle.

C **PULL-DOWN:** Most popular style, with gooseneck spout. The head of the faucet comes out attached to a hose. This style is best for deep and/or big sinks.

D **WATER FILTRATION SYSTEMS:** This is something to consider early on, as it will most likely be incorporated next to your sink area, if not in your fridge, and will require an extra hole in the countertop.

E **POT-FILLERS:** Typically installed in the stove area, these are designed to swivel out when in use and sit back relatively flush against the wall when not in use.

BEYOND THE KITCHEN SINK

Don't miss these opportunities for installing running water when renovating.

1 **LAUNDRY SINK:** A narrow profile with an extra deep basin contains splashes and leaves room for sorting and folding in the laundry room.

2 **MUDROOM SINK:** Pair a sleek undermount with a similarly-colored backsplash for an almost invisible workstation that keeps outdoor messes from making their way too far into the house.

3 WET BAR: The cutest of the bunch, a petite wet bar sink makes easy work of rinsing glasses and other barware.

THE BATHROOM SINK

When choosing a sink, think about how often you'll use it and how much space you'll need. Otherwise, it's a matter of preference. Consider these styles:

1 **SELF RIMMING (OR "DROP-IN"):** This style has a finishing rim that makes it easy and cheap to install and replace, since the cutout can look unfinished and the rim will cover it up.

2 **UNDERMOUNT:** Installed from the underside of a countertop, these sinks require that your cutout be customized to the exact size and shape of your sink.

3 **VESSEL:** The bowl sits atop the counter with this style of sink. Design-wise, they can be hard to use, given the high edge. Consider them for lesser-used powder rooms.

4 **PEDESTAL:** A vintage-inspired, classic look that's especially great for a powder room. It's a beautiful shape, but you get no storage beneath the sink.

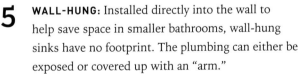

5   **WALL-HUNG:** Installed directly into the wall to help save space in smaller bathrooms, wall-hung sinks have no footprint. The plumbing can either be exposed or covered up with an "arm."

6   **VANITY:** This all-in-one is composed of a countertop and sink. If your vanity unit does not come with a cabinet base, get one that is 1 inch smaller than the countertop for some overhang.

7 **CONSOLE:** A sink that is supported by two or four legs, console sinks have little or no counter space, similar to that of a pedestal sink, though the actual basin is larger. With consoles you want to consider matching the finish of your faucet to the plumbing (P trap and/or supply lines), since they will be exposed below.

8 **FLOATING:** This legless vanity can be ready-made and recessed into the wall or customized to run wall to wall. If made out of stone it can be pricey, but the contemporary look is striking.

This vanity might look like a solid piece of marble, but it's not. It's built out of wood and then faced with marble and mitered edges. We leathered the stone to give it a more natural look.

BATHTUB INSTALLATION TYPES

While tub styles are all about how you want to feel when settling in for a soak, where your plumbing is located and bathroom square footage are important factors, too.

1 **ALCOVE:** With one finished side and three other sides that serve as your walls or "surround," this is the easiest option to replace if the need arises.

2 **FREESTANDING:** A sculpture in the middle of your bathroom. Detached from the walls, these can take up more floor space but stylistically they make quite the spa statement.

3 **DROP-IN:** Also known as "platform tubs," drop-ins are only the shell of the tub, which is placed in a wooden frame for support and then finished off in a material of your choosing.

4 **UNDERMOUNT:** Although installation (and the high price tag) is similar to drop-in styles, the difference here is that the top or "deck" of the tub is covered with another material, such as tile or stone.

TUB SPOUTS

To switch the water flow between your showerhead and tub spout, you'll either have a diverter built into the spout, or a valve controlled by a handle on the wall. Spouts are typically installed in one of three ways:

1 **TUB FILLER:** Paired with freestanding tubs, this spout is elongated by a tube that is separate from the tub itself; they sometimes come equipped with a handheld shower wand as well.

2 **WALL-MOUNTED:** This is a very common style, making it easier to pair with the rest of your shower suite.

3 **DECK-MOUNTED:** This installation method can be used with freestanding tubs, as well as drop-in or alcove styles.

hot tip To help you decide where to install the bathtub fixtures, think about your head placement (and which way you want to face while soaking).

PART 2
—
PUT IT
INTO
PRACTICE

IN THE KITCHEN

If you are getting ready to take on a kitchen renovation or an update, I want to reach out of this book and give you a big hug, as you're probably going to need it. I know I did.

Renovating the kitchen is where you'll likely spend the most money and feel the most stress, but, ultimately, it is also where you will pass the most time (living room aside). No wonder they call it the heart of the home. It's also the space that will add the most value to your property in the long term, which requires that you make some pretty big, very permanent decisions.

If you have a vintage home, you might consider the layout—moving or removing walls to open up tight spaces and make the room more easily navigable. But that not only costs you money, it also takes time, during which you'll be faced with lots of takeout nights. Until you can achieve your dream kitchen, you might be just as happy with a simple update. Consider buying new appliances, repainting cabinets, replacing uppers with open shelving, and even adding a new backsplash and countertop.

So many decisions—no pressure! I'm here to help you through it.

LAYING OUT THE KITCHEN

Let's begin with how your kitchen is set up, or how you want it to be set up. More specifically, where does everything in your kitchen live? Most designers default to **THE KITCHEN TRIANGLE RULE**, which puts three main appliances—the sink, refrigerator, and the stove—all in, you guessed it, a triangle. This often obsessed-over layout was invented to make cooking easy and efficient, but there are many scenarios I've been in where this rule was better off broken.

So if the triangle isn't the be-all and end-all of kitchen layouts, how else might you consider arranging your cooking space? I'm glad you asked.

BEFORE YOU LAND ON A KITCHEN LAYOUT, CONSIDER:

HOW MUCH DO YOU TRULY COOK? If you are more of a "make food from scratch" type, then you will have different layout needs than a quick cook.

ARE THERE OFTEN MULTIPLE COOKS? If so, you'll want to make sure that you aren't on top of each other.

DO YOU ENTERTAIN A LOT? Think about where you want guests to hang and whether it makes sense to keep your island free of a stovetop or sink so there's room for a cheese board instead.

DO YOU HAVE KIDS? If so, then prioritize storage. Give yourself a large pantry and reserve those lower drawers for everyday plates and glassware so the kids can help themselves.

WILL YOUR ISLAND BE USED FOR EATING? Or would you prefer a small kitchen table that doubles as a homework station for the kids? (Hey there, breakfast nook.)

HOW CLEAR DO YOU LIKE YOUR COUNTERTOPS? This is where you might consider an appliance garage and easy access to oils, spices, and cooking tools. Let's find a hidden (yet convenient) place for everything.

LAND YOUR ULTIMATE LAYOUT:

The three most popular kitchen layouts include the open concept, the galley, and the U-shaped.

OPEN CONCEPT: Who needs boundaries? The reigning layout for decades, open concept kitchens allow for easy flow to the living spaces. But this layout is starting to fall out of favor because of its lack of privacy. It's also hard to hide messes.

GALLEY: A more traditional layout, the galley is starting to trend again with folks wanting more separation between spaces. If you love to cook with all the things, then the galley might be for you with two walls where you can stash a ton of cabinets. Think about adding a skylight or a window, or opening up one end of the kitchen to keep the space from feeling too dark.

THE U: With three walls for your cabinets and appliances, this might be the Goldilocks of layouts. Work that kitchen triangle to your advantage, gain more floor space, and enjoy some privacy while still feeling connected to the rest of the home.

CLEVER STORAGE SOLUTIONS

ABOVE: Install a spice drawer at eye level, you don't have to lean over while cooking.

ABOVE LEFT: Hang your most beloved utensils above your stove for easy access (and style).

LEFT: Go shallow with shelving for soup cans and condiments by installing them on the inside of cabinet panels.

OPPOSITE: More and more, lower cabinets are making way for deep drawers, made so you can see everything and access cookware more easily. Just make sure they are deep enough to hold your mixing bowls and stockpots.

RIGHT: Unused wall space could feature art, but why not make it more functional with shallow shelving that can house canisters, oils, and utensils.

BELOW: A narrow space can still hold a lot of function, and leaving a space open gives you a fun styling opportunity.

BOTTOM RIGHT: Introduce another material and provide more storage with an under-cabinet shelf. It instantly makes this kitchen look more custom (and functional). And don't forget the back of your cabinets or shelves—this affordable caning detail adds texture and depth.

The first stage of designing your cabinetry should be locating and placing everything you need and use frequently. Write on your drawings what you are putting where to ensure you have a designated spot for your oils, for instance.

COLOR YOUR CABINETS

Picking the right finish for your kitchen cabinets is like getting engaged. It's not a permanent commitment, but reversing your decision can be expensive—and likely to cause tears. That doesn't mean you shouldn't be daring and fearless in your choices, however. Bold, modern paint is one approach, but there are other ideas you should consider.

PAINTED UNIFORM

A bold or airy wash of a single color can be stunning on both modern and traditional kitchen cabinets. Take the paint from floor to ceiling, paint your island a different hue, and play around with the hardware to keep it from looking boring.

PAINTED TWO-TONED

Mix colors across the island, wall, and cabinetry. This can be a modern touch in a home with older bones and works especially well in a monochrome color scheme. A tuxedo look—light on top, dark on the bottom—can make a kitchen feel bigger at eye level, without committing to a whole room of color.

MIXED FINISHES

Break up the finish in the same run of cabinets. This technique is unusual, but when executed intentionally— say, painting just the sink cabinet or the drawers and leaving the cabinet exteriors natural—it looks so custom.

hot tip If working with real wood consider staining a color instead of painting. A black stain will have the same dark color, but show more grain and texture than paint.

A large multiuse island has enough space for eat-in dining or entertaining at one end and prep surface and sink at the other.

HAVE FUN WITH HARDWARE

My approach to hardware is similar to putting together an outfit: If cabinets are the clothes, the hardware is the jewelry, and thus gives the finishing touches to the entire look. That said, the choice of bringing in that pop of shine or skipping it altogether for a more minimal look will mostly be informed by the style of your kitchen. More traditional designs lend themselves to prominent hardware, while modern kitchens are a good match for slimmer pulls or none at all. (Think: Scandinavian style, where you have a carved lip or finger hole instead of a handle, or you push the door to open it.)

You don't just choose a knob or handle and be done with it. You first and foremost have to think about function: How will you be positioned when you pull open that drawer or reach for that cupboard? What will that drawer contain? From there, you need to scale your handles to the size of your drawers.

HOW TO DO HARDWARE RIGHT

CHANGE UP THE HANDLE TYPES. You aren't beholden to one or another—a combination of knobs on cabinets and pulls on drawers makes a kitchen look custom and far more interesting. Latches are a sweet and decorative option, but they're less easy to open, so best to save them for pieces you don't need such easy access to.

MIX YOUR METALS. The secret to nailing this look is changing up the metal finishes on different surfaces. If you do it intentionally and evenly throughout the space, you're all good. For example, choose one type of metal for the upper cabinet run and a different one for the island lowers. You can also mix painted wooden knobs with metal handles, and I'd recommend having the knobs painted the same color, so the cabinets don't get too busy-looking and the metal hardware can pop a bit more.

CHOOSE THE RIGHT SIZE. When buying handles, think about the sizes of the hands in your household. If someone in your house has big paws, go for at least a five-inch handle so they won't have to squeeze their ample fingers into a tiny three-inch gap.

GET THE RIGHT PULL FOR THE JOB. These days many people are opting to integrate their appliances, such as a refrigerator or a dishwasher, into their kitchens by hiding them behind custom cabinetry fronts. For this look, you'll need a height-weight pull to handle the weight of constantly opening and closing the door, especially given the load that the suction of a fridge will create. Go for a handle that coordinates with the rest of your hardware.

SCALE YOUR HANDLES TO YOUR DRAWER OR DOOR. You also want to orient your handles based on their function. It's easier to pull the spice drawer out with a horizontal handle; it doesn't matter that the other drawers might feature handles in a vertical orientation.

POSITION KNOBS AND PULLS IN THE RIGHT PLACE. There are a million different ways to position handles, but it comes down to ease and convenience for each one. Just be consistent. If you have shaker panels keep the hardware in the corners on cabinets and in the middle on drawers.

pro tip If you are replacing your cabinet hardware, make sure to measure from hole to hole, not from end to end, to determine the "spread," which is what tells you what to shop for. For example, "five inches" typically refers to the length of a handle from hole to hole.

CABINET HARDWARE: A CASE STUDY

Going into this kitchen reno in Portland, Oregon, I was on the hunt for the perfect mix of contrasts: classic plus modern, happy plus sophisticated, and contemporary plus timeless. I also wanted enough thoughtful moments to make the space feel really, really *special*. The details we landed on make it hard to pick a favorite—I love them all!—but I learned so much from this project about the true impact of hardware.

Originally, I was going to do polished nickel hardware to match the range and faucets, but the more I stared at the materials board, the more I craved the warmth and modern feel of brass. I found myself circling back to my own design rule about mixing metals (see page 226). I brought in four different styles and sizes, all in the same finish, from Portland's own Rejuvenation hardware store. The effect is truly sophisticated and unlike anything we'd get had we gone with a single handle style.

CLOCKWISE FROM TOP LEFT:
Cabinet door latch, appliance pull, drawer handle, knob.

CONSIDER THE ISLAND

Once your kitchen foundation is all set, it's time to drop your anchor—the island. This is your moment to contrast that wall of cabinetry in a way that makes your kitchen feel special and custom (unless you want a streamlined look that matches). Mix up the color and the material, and even add some decorative details like legs, beadboard, and, my personal dream, a shoe railing and my very own bag hook.

Here's how to maximize your island's true potential, both functionally and aesthetically.

FURNITURE-STYLE

Freestanding islands with furniture-style legs are worth considering if you're looking to incorporate some old-world charm into your kitchen in a modern way. But though it can make your space feel bigger, you sacrifice storage and the ability to put a cooktop, or sink, or dishwasher there. Plus, it's harder to sweep underneath.

MULTIFUNCTIONAL

Half enclosed, to house cabinetry and appliances, these islands are typically bigger and ideally have ample room for in-kitchen dining. They're a nice alternative to a breakfast nook and a great option for dinner party hosts who don't mind early guests joining them in the kitchen while they keep an eye on their soufflé. To keep the look current, don't break up the counter with a higher breakfast bar. This bygone style was designed originally to provide a sense of separation—like, "I cook, you drink"— but they create an awkward break visually, limit the way you can use the countertop. Try mixing materials and finishes instead, to create zones for cooking and perching.

rule breaker Don't be afraid to install a prep sink on a furniture style island like Architect William Hunt did. The exposed copper pipes add a salvaged edgy vibe.

ENCLOSED AND ENCASED TO THE FLOOR

This streamlined look provides the most storage and can house cooktops and undercounter microwaves. But if you want your island to double as an entertaining space, the absence of barstools might be a dealbreaker.

THE WATERFALL

Use the same stone on both the top and sides of your island for a statement effect, especially if the stone features natural, dramatic veining. You probably won't get the same impact with engineered stone, unless you opt for white quartz with a faux veining, which is an equally pretty and more budget-friendly option.

PRECEDING PAGES, LEFT: Before the "kitchen island" we had "kitchen tables," which floated in the kitchen and acted as prep space as well as dinner service. What you lose in storage you gain in unexpected old-world vibes, which is especially welcome in an older home.

PRECEDING PAGES, RIGHT: A brass-clad wraparound island houses drawers on one side and stools on the other—a truly glamorous and wildly unexpected design choice.

ABOVE RIGHT: Here's a genius way to store dry goods that is as chic as it is functional. Velinda Hellen utilized a brass rail to show off these pantry staples.

BOTTOM RIGHT: For a really contemporary and streamlined look, you can go with the same cabinetry and countertops on the island; using wood and stone gives you a lot of texture.

hot tip You typically want 12 to 16 inches of overhang of countertop for pulling up a stool. And make sure you buy counter-height stools, not bar-height.

CONSIDER THE COUNTERTOPS

Choosing the right countertops *may* give you flashbacks to high school earth science class, but I promise you, you don't need a geology degree to pick the best one.

ABOVE: A natural stone countertop calls for natural materials: wood shelves and bamboo-wrapped accessories. The pink tile keeps this look casual and stylish.

BOTTOM RIGHT: Designer Carly Waters chose quartz countertops from Caesarstone, which are a durable and sustainable choice and don't sacrifice any style.

OPPOSITE: Honed marble features stunning veins, which add texture and depth (and also hide inevitable use).

BELOW: A DIY butcher block top was constructed to sit on top of the dated tile counter in Jess' rental kitchen.

MAKE A (BACK) SPLASH

Whichever material you choose for your backsplash, you need at least four inches, but feel free to take it all the way up to the ceiling or even match the height of your cabinetry.

LEFT: Ending the backsplash with a peg rail is such a simple and yet useful way to not only cap something off, but provide more function and styling opportunities.

ABOVE: For a more minimal look and to save on tiling, simply take the counter material up the wall six inches. Just be sure to check where it interacts with your light switches, outlets, and windows.

BOTTOM LEFT: A custom backsplash, designed by Kassina Folstad, is a truly stunning piece of art. While wood isn't ideal for a backsplash, if sealed (and resealed) properly and added to a low-use bathroom, it can hold up nicely.

While six inches is the minimum for a backsplash, feel free to take it up the whole wall. In this case, Victoria Sass made a statement with marble, covering even the sconce. Well done.

LIGHT THE KITCHEN

Bravo on making it through the massive kitchen undertaking. But before you pour your glass of bubbly, there's one more thing we need to talk about: lighting.

In the kitchen, your choices are simpler. You need overhead lighting, such as cans, recessed fixtures, or track lighting to create an evenly and brightly lit cooking space. Then you have optional lighting, like over the sink and island fixtures, which could be in the form of sconces or pendants. These are nice to have when you don't want to turn on overhead lights, and you're aiming for softer ambience. Undercabinet lighting also falls into the optional budget, but it could roll over into necessary territory if you tend to make nighttime runs to the fridge.

An easy way to think of all your decorative kitchen lighting is that the lights should look like they belong in the same house and have something in common—whether style, color, or finish. But the shape and function can vary.

hot tip   Keep the ceiling lights (track or recessed) on the same switch, but allow your pendants or sconces to function separately from them to have a less "clinical" ambiance after you're done cooking and cleaning. Trust me, you don't want just one big on and off switch, and you should give yourself some dimming options.

A single sconce over the sink contrasts nicely with the multi-light ceiling fixture. Together they bring a classic yet eclectic look to this kitchen.

ABOVE: Let the outlets pick up the finish of nearby lighting fixtures or cabinetry hardware.

ABOVE RIGHT: With their elegant, unassuming charm, these Edison bulb pendants add a quiet drama to this minimalist kitchen.

RIGHT: Twins, with mini-mes. These four lights are the same finish and style, but the smaller ones are scaled appropriately over the counter so as not to block the window.

LEFT: Note how the pendant and the semi-flush-mounted light in this kitchen have different finishes, but they correspond to the hardware and fixtures found on the surfaces below them. Mix-and-match perfection!

ABOVE: For high-impact lighting, repeat three times and make sure to center the middle light over the sink.

hot tip It's perfectly acceptable to mix two different stones in a single space. For example, marble and limestone are lovely together. Just make sure your two choices contrast enough so they don't compete with each other; let the busier stone take center stage.

IN THE BATHROOM

If you've ever tackled a kitchen reno, much of what you learned from the experience can be applied here. That said, a bathroom is its own beast—albeit a smaller one—because this little room has to work really hard. It is, in essence, the office where your family's morning meetings are held, a makeshift ER when you need to perform triage on a knee scrape, and, of course, your private quarters where you get to relax and release.

Every bathroom consists of a few building blocks. No matter which template you're working with, you already know the three key elements: a vanity, tub and/or shower, and toilet. And I'd add a few more: lighting, floors, and walls. Tying these elements together is where a little interior design expertise comes in handy, and that expert could just as well be you, your GC (see page 12), or, in many cases, a dedicated kitchen and bath designer employed by your hardware vendor or contracting firm (see page 15).

CHOOSING A VANITY

The number one thing to consider when choosing a vanity (your sink, countertop, and cabinet combo, sometimes referred to as a lavatory) is size and proportion in relation to your bathroom's square footage. Like kitchen cabinetry, you can go the off-the-shelf route, in which case you're looking at a "counter height" vanity, measuring roughly 36 inches tall. For a long time, bathroom vanities were typically 30 to 32 inches tall, or you can add something more custom—whether a flea market find or your own unique design.

On pages 103–105, I've covered everything you need to know about the two most popular hard surfaces: tile, the OG of bathroom countertops and a relatively easy DIY project, and natural stone, the sure bet if you're aiming for a spa-like bathroom experience. But here's the quick-and-dirty on two other options you might find to be a better fit for your lifestyle and budget: quartz (which is very durable, but not heat resistant) and porcelain (which is durable *and* heat resistant for those who rely on hair straighteners and curling irons).

hot tip Buy your vanity before you buy a faucet. In fact, the vanity cabinet you choose, and the height at which you install it, will inform the style and size not only of your faucet, but also of your mirror or medicine cabinet, sconces, and other lighting as well.

ABOVE RIGHT: An antique dresser gets repurposed as a vanity with some custom woodworking.

RIGHT: A simply designed double vanity can fit a variety of styles.

rule breaker (above) A custom vanity is offset, with only one sink on the left to make space for a proper face prep zone. Please note that they took the mirror all the way to the floor.

ABOVE LEFT: A wall-mounted vanity adds a seamless and airy feel to the bath.

LEFT: A vanity with front legs adds a touch of tradition (and some ease of installation when wall-mounted might be too complicated).

BY THE NUMBERS

32 TO 36 INCHES: Height of vanity, pedestal, or console sink.

21 TO 30 INCHES: Clearance in front of vanity, tub, and toilet.

24 TO 30 INCHES: Clearance between vanity and bathtub or shower.

5 TO 10 INCHES: Distance between bottom of mirror and sink.

60 TO 72 INCHES: Height of vanity sconces (or install them at eye level).

36 TO 40 INCHES: Distance between vanity sconces for optimal lighting.

75 TO 77 INCHES: Height of shower curtain rod from the floor.

LEFT: FYI, while this floating vanity looks like it's made of solid stone, there is a frame made out of wood underneath it, attached solidly to the wall (often with metal supports), and the stone is simply set on top.

OPPOSITE: Drawer pulls don't have to "pop" off the drawers; a finger pull in the same tone as the drawers disappears and recedes, while still tying in with the faucet.

pro tip While the numbers are here to guide us, it's important to stand in front of a vanity and get a feel for what you like (your height makes a difference). What you want to avoid is not being able to see your face easily in the mirror and having bright bulbs installed right at eye level. Know the rules, but please creatively break them.

THE GREAT
MEDICINE CABINET DEBATE

Choosing whether to have a medicine cabinet ranks among the most controversial bathroom decisions among designers, believe it or not. Let me explain why I've never been a fan:

1

They can look generic. I'm not saying they always are, but most ready-made ones don't make my heart sing. (Is there a hole in the market? Yes.)

2

Their frames are often too big and chunky. This is likely due to the weight of the cabinet itself, but it's often not the look I'm going for.

3

Inset/recessed versions require wall construction, and that's scary if you aren't really into something for the long run.

4

The good ones are really expensive, but can be worth it.

5

Wall-mounted medicine cabinets can eat up real estate, which isn't great in small spaces.

That said, there's still one very good reason to keep with tradition and install a medicine cabinet: extra storage. If wall construction isn't for you, opt for a statement mirror—what I like to think of as the artwork of the bathroom. And install it so you have roughly 64 inches from the floor to the mirror's center.

A vanity with a cabinet underneath or a freestanding armoire or linen closet is the most practical, multipurpose solution. A great DIY hack is to recess the cabinet (simple shallow shelves will do), find a vintage mirror the right size, and add hinges to one edge. With some careful measuring and handiwork, mount it as your medicine cabinet. You now have hidden storage in such a chic way.

OPPOSITE: If you're lucky enough to have a vintage bathroom like this, embrace the quirk with some simple, tasteful updates. They don't make bathrooms like this anymore.

ABOVE RIGHT: Who says farmhouse sinks are just for kitchens? This one is framed by a gorgeous custom wood console and pull-out drawers, and an antique wall-mounted brass faucet.

OPPOSITE: Enhance vintage tile by painting the wall color a moody tone of the same color. The results feel modern and fresh without changing the intentions of the space.

BOTTOM RIGHT: This ultra-thick countertop was mitered together to look thick, but is actually not—smart design with a lot of heft.

ABOVE: A dark blue stone is an unexpected choice for a powder room and is SO good.

hot tip Consider a window in your shower/bathtub area. As long as it's high enough (for privacy) it will bring in so much light, making the bathroom feel bigger.

THE PROS AND CONS OF
PEDESTAL SINKS

Pedestal and console sinks get major points for freeing up physical and visual space—they're a great option for small spaces or powder baths, where the storage of a vanity cabinet is neither needed or nor feasible. But their biggest drawback is their lack of built-in storage and countertop space. If you go with this look, baskets, shelving, and towel hooks will give you the functionality you need to stash your stuff. This could be an opportunity for hidden or inset shelving.

If you aren't doing a full bathroom reno but want to swap out a vanity for a pedestal or console sink, keep in mind that the floor and wall might not be finished behind the vanity cabinet. Be sure to account for any repairs needed— like replacing and painting drywall or matching floor tiles—before you rip out the old cabinet and begin.

Jamie Haller brought drama to this powder room in her Craftsman home with a deeply hued wainscoting and penny tile, and wallpaper that has a nostalgic feel.

THE FIXTURES

Speaking of finishes, your plumbing fixtures, from sink to shower, and accessories, like your towel bar and toilet paper holder, should look like they match. To that end, the same finish is crucial.

The common denominator, even when it comes to finishes, is the overall style of your space. If you have a more contemporary home, for example, then matte black might be the right finish for your hardware and fixtures. If your home is more traditional, then polished nickel or brass could work well. But also consider the other metals that you'll want to work into the design of your room.

GO UNIVERSAL

Keep ADA (American Disabilities Act) complacency in mind for your home with these faucet handles that work for everyone:

LEVER: The most common, this design is typical for a three-hole sink and is easy for children and elderly to use.

SINGLE: A single handle controls both hot and cold temperatures and is easy to use. This style can be installed on single or two-hole sinks.

MOTION/TOUCH: Though rarely used in residence bathrooms, this design helps with water conservation.

BATHTUBS

The tub is a *major* bathroom consideration, not just because of the amount of real estate it takes up, but because of how integral it is to your daily routine. In choosing one, think about what kind of "experience" you want to have there. Are you the five-minute, shower-only type? Or are you looking to do some serious soaking with salts and steam and all of the bells and whistles? Or maybe bath time isn't as much of a luxury for you as it is for your kids, in which case practicality will be the priority. Either way, size, cost, style, material, and weight will also factor into your decision. Here's what you need to know.

TYPES OF BATHTUBS

STANDARD: Five feet long by 30 inches wide by 14 to 16 inches high (alcove, freestanding, or drop-in) on average, the standard is the most affordable option.

SOAKING: Typically the same width and length of a standard tub but much deeper, so you can fully submerge. Prices run from $300 into the thousands depending on the style and material.

WHIRLPOOL: Includes jets to target large muscle groups and relieve joint pressure in a massage-like way.

AIR: Instead of a few concentrated jets, these tubs disperse the air more evenly to create a relaxing, effervescent atmosphere.

WALK-IN: Typically used by people who need better accessibility, this style often has a "door" and a seat feature built in.

hot tip To rejuvenate an old bathtub and extend its life, you can have it reglazed or refinished. But you may find replacing it a better use of your money.

THE SURROUND

As the name implies, a tub surround is the term used to describe the surfaces above and around your bathtub that help keep water from seeping into your walls. It's recommended that your surround extend at least 3 inches above the showerhead rough-in or to a minimum height of 72 inches above the finished floor.

And though they're primarily functional, tub surrounds can have a major impact aesthetically, acting as a backdrop to your fixtures and tub, and, in some cases, providing stash spots for bath time candles or toiletries.

Flooring is going to play a supporting role in whichever tub surround you choose, particularly if it's also made of tile, so lay out the materials alongside each other before you make a decision. You might also consider your vanity countertop in this equation to ensure that it feels cohesive and complementary once installed in the same space.

If you choose a wood apron for your bathtub be sure to have your stone extend at least half an inch to avoid constant moisture on the wood. If it's a heavily used bath (that sees lots of kids), opt for tile fronts or freestanding.

rule breaker Consider a wall-mount faucet for a freestanding tub versus a roman tub or floor mount faucet. It's chic (but note that you might miss the hand shower).

SHOWERS

The best showerheads deliver three things: a strong flow, steady temperature, and a selection of sprays. Whether you rent or own your home, a new showerhead is an easy way to customize your bathroom.

TYPES OF SHOWERHEADS

SINGLE SPRAY. Most common and affordable, single sprays give you great water pressure but can be difficult to use when washing children and pets.

DUAL. Also in the affordable range, these multifunctional fixtures offer the best of both worlds: rain shower (relaxation factor) and handheld (functional factor). Sizing of the fixture itself is a large part of the selection process. You'll need to consider the shower size and make sure the scale of your fixture is proportionate. Dual showerheads typically feature a lever that allows you to switch how the water sprays out for different uses. For example: rain, massage, water-saving mist, rain/massage, and rain/mist.

RAIN. Though they're a luxury touch, rain showers tend to waste a lot of water and sometimes don't have enough pressure to properly wash your hair (especially if you're blessed with luscious locks). The reason why? Water usage regulations, which are federally mandated and dependent on state. Many come with a 2.5 gallons per minute or less flow. New York, California, and Colorado have a standard 2.0 gpm flow rate, for reference.

CEILING MOUNT. Installed into the ceiling itself with no flange, these showerheads disperse water evenly in a straight-down direction, leaving surrounding areas drier than other types. They're easy to clean but can be hard to install. Avoid this type of fixture if you live in an area with a lower flow rate, as they don't work as well when the water pressure is low.

HANDHELD. These fixtures are a great choice when you have pets, children, or target areas to clean. They can also help you use less water and save you money in the long run.

LOW WATER PRESSURE. A more expensive option, these fixtures balance water pressure to efficiently get you clean.

SHOWER PANELS. This more modern look can be costly but is generally low-maintenance. They may include all of the fixture types—showerhead, handheld, and body sprays—in one system.

SLIDING BAR. Typically paired with a handheld showerhead, this option is great for families who share one bath because it allows each member to adjust it to their optimal height.

We love a shower "ledge" versus the "niche." It's more streamlined and doesn't interrupt the tile wall as much (plus it gives you a chance to rotate the tile direction).

SHOWER DRAINS

Whether or not you have a shower curb, you need to have the proper slope on your shower threshold. When installed correctly, water will shed down the glass door, land on the sloped curb, and shed toward the drain and not onto your bathroom floor.

Point drains are most common. They sit in the center of your sloped shower floor, drawing in water from all four sides like a funnel. Their shape can either be round or square. The latter is great when using tile that is also squared off, allowing you to avoid unnecessary cuts (more cuts equals more money). But you shouldn't use tiles larger than 4 inches by 4 inches in size.

Linear drains, on the other hand, are a long and narrow style that has gained popularity recently. They are positioned on the opposite wall from the shower entrance with the shower floor, sloping one way in that direction. Occasionally, they are placed in the center of the shower, but that is rare and typically used only in very large shower areas. Since they can go up to 72 inches in length, they're good to pair with larger tile (12 inch size), which will give you a seamless look with the rest of the bathroom floor.

The last step in selecting a drain style is picking a grate (the part that is seen). If you go with a metal finish, make sure to match the finish to the rest of your fixture suite. A tileable grate is a wonderful option if you want the drain to disappear. The water will drain around the edges of the grate.

hot tip If you decide to install a high-end feature like a steam shower, know that it requires the entire surround to be completely closed off and tiled or otherwise waterproofed, including the ceiling. If you have high ceilings, this might not be the best option, since some glass door manufacturers have a height limit.

WHAT'S THE DEAL WITH
CURBLESS SHOWERS?

Shower curbs, the "dam" or "curb," which is the step-up part of the shower opening that prevents water from running out, are not required, but when they are incorporated into a shower design, there are requirements for how they must be installed.

Curbs must be at least 2 inches higher than the drain, but not more than 9 inches higher.

For curbless showers, the floor-level threshold at the opening serves the same purpose. It is where visible water will escape and limit the rise of water up the walls.

There's no ignoring this black beauty of a bath. Corbett Tuck designed a curbless shower complete with a steel and glass door and marble featuring the most dramatic veining. The door keeps the shower open to the rest of the bathroom, but when closed it creates a spa-like steam shower.

YOUR CHOICE: GLASS OR CURTAIN

Like most of the design choices you'll make throughout your home, choosing between a glass panel or door and a curtain comes down to where form and function net out in your specific situation. Glass panels provide a clean, modern aesthetic but could also look a bit cold, given all of the other hard surfaces in the bathroom. A shower "room" means that the shower is fully enclosed in its own walls, except for a door, of course, which is often glass. This can make your room look smaller, but it gives more privacy as well as a cozy feel.

Curtains, on the other hand, can add a layer of warmth, pattern, and color. Their ability to quickly slide back and forth allow for easier access to the tub. To keep the look high-end, hang your curtain on a fixed rod that matches the other finishes in the room.

hot tip Most shower curtains are 72 inches long, and you want to hang the rod high enough to float your curtain a few inches off the ground so it doesn't get wet.

This original clawfoot tub was salvaged and repainted black, making it feel fresh, modern, and yet totally appropriate for the vintage house.

DON'T FORGET THE DETAILS

Yes, you're going to be making a lot of *major* design decisions throughout your home, but trust me when I say that the smallest changes often make the biggest difference in how special it all feels. As you think through the finishing touches of this room, here is some inspiration to keep in mind.

LEFT: Make creative use of a deck-mount installation, such as on a ledge that can serve as a surface for other items (ahem, a glass of wine).

ABOVE: Consider varying the scale of a similar tile pattern from one room to the next—you'll announce the room transition while sticking with the design theme.

IN THE LIVING ROOMS

Welcome to the rooms that exist for our sheer enjoyment and relaxation. Back in the day, you had two options (if that): the formal living room with plastic-covered furniture and the well-loved, albeit neglected, fully carpeted family room. Thankfully, we've made the shift to caring for these rooms equally.

The difference between these rooms is really just who's hanging out there, how you want to use the room, and most importantly the vibe you're going for. And you know how I feel about creating a good vibe.

Maybe you have only one room for your living space. In that case it has to work even harder. Your living room is the most guest-facing of your rooms—your house's business card, so to speak. Creating one that is functional, comfortable, and interesting isn't as easy as even I like to think it is. I have struggled so hard to create a living space that is cool enough to impress our guests while also serving as our family room. I've learned A LOT.

LET'S HANG OUT

Because we spend so much time at home, I am personally a proponent of giving the living rooms enough purpose that you actually spend time in them. If it's a living room, design it to be *lived* in; if it's a family or media room, let your family really use it (go for that big TV!), and if it's a den or basement family room, design it for maximum coziness ready for cuddling and hibernation. With my two kids and pups, every room is a family room in my house, and that's how we like it.

Most of the design tips in this chapter apply to any sofa-related space, and we've included some tweaks and tips specific to how each room will be used. The existential questions: What is this room's purpose? What pulls you in and makes you want to stay for a while?

Visualizing how you will use your great room will help you not only choose the type of furniture to bring in but also know where it all should go.

Sara Liggoria-Tramp wanted to add entryway storage to her long, narrow living room, so she positioned the sofa perpendicular to the fireplace to keep the front door clear.

HOW TO ARRANGE FURNITURE

In general, your goal is to promote conversation while optimizing the flow and focal points of the space. You want your furniture close enough together to make it easy to, yes, converse while still allowing folks to engage with the whole room.

1
FIND YOUR FOCAL POINT (OR CREATE ONE).

It sounds easy enough to locate the most prominent feature in the room— the fireplace or TV, typically— but for many rooms there may be no clear focal point. Or there might be more than one (true story), which makes orienting a room more difficult.

My suggestion: *Sit and stare.* What do you want to look at? In our living room, everyone thought that we should have the sofa face the fireplace, but when in the room, you just wanted to look out the beautiful windows to a backyard of trees. So we chose to orient the sofa toward the windows instead. It's hard to know the focal point until you are in the room and you realize, "Yes, this is how I want to sit." You don't necessarily have to face the focal point; you can just arrange your furniture around it.

2
START WITH YOUR ANCHOR.

Because you have to start somewhere, figure out what your anchor will be, which is the largest piece of furniture or decor in the room that will determine everything else. This will likely be your sofa, but it can also be your rug. Figure out where that piece should land and start building out from there.

3
THINK ABOUT BALANCE, FLOW, AND SCALE.

These are the technical terms that designers have to think about (and for good reason), but nothing needs to be perfect. Here are a few handy ways to achieve a layout trifecta:

SCALE. Your furniture should match the size of your room. So a large living room often needs a large sectional, but here's a shocker: A large sectional can *also* work in a small living room— situate it in a corner and the room actually feels bigger. If your sofa is big, then you might think the armchair needs to be too, but a pair of small-scale chairs visually create one large chair. When pairing seating, choose seat heights that are within 4 inches of each other.

BALANCE. The easiest way to think about balance is by looking at whether the visual weight of the room is equally distributed, both in color and in furniture/seating. This just means that things should feel close to equal visually. It could be a big painting that balances out a sofa, or a bench that balances out two club chairs.

FLOW. Your room should be easy to navigate from one end to the other. Make sure you have enough space for your walkways and to get to where you want to go. You don't want guests bumping their knees when they get up from the couch or having to squeeze past a side table on their way out. This might involve a bit of trial and error, so don't be afraid to arrange and rearrange your pieces.

LAYING IT OUT

Pairing furniture can be hard. You have to consider colors, styles, fabrics, and, most importantly, scale, all of which can be confusing and overwhelming. Here are some common layouts and the furniture pieces you need to make them work.

1 **TWO FACING SOFAS:** For equal opportunity lounging, go for double sofas—either exactly the same or very similar in style and fabric.

2 **SOFA FACING TWO CHAIRS:** Here's a versatile option that will allow you to move seating around. Scale everything appropriately—you want to avoid petite chairs with one massive sofa.

3 **A SOFA + SETTEE/BENCH + CORNER CHAIR:** If you've got the space, add a settee or a bench and set it off to the side for occasional seating. Consider a slimmer silhouette to avoid having too many heavy pieces in the room.

4 **SECTIONAL + ONE OR TWO ACCENT CHAIRS:** Adding a few more seats to your L-shaped sectional will complete the conversation pit. Pro move: adding a pouf adds some comfort to the chairs, while helping you out in case of a seating emergency.

hot tip Measure and tape it out. Yes, designers use fancy floor plan programs, but honestly, we also just take blue tape and tape out the shape and size of the sofa, rug, and chairs in your room. It's one of the most accurate ways to know it will fit.

5 **SECTIONAL + ONE ACCENT CHAIR:** A good combo that creates a conversation area and gives some separation, but provides so much seating.

6 **TWO SOFAS PERPENDICULAR TO EACH OTHER:**
A great set-up for family rooms where there's a TV
or a living room with a special fireplace, you might
want to orient the sofas so everyone can face the
focal point.

A small ottoman and taller side table create a unique nesting table that has two functions and also looks very cool.

LET'S TALK TV

I take TV watching seriously in our family room, but forgo it in the living room. But to each family their own. Whatever helps you actually enjoy your home is what you should do. Again, because space is at a premium, avoid an unused living room at all costs.

Generally, the TV should be about seven feet away from the sofa and should be placed around seated eye level, which is three feet six inches. But sometimes you may not have that perfect wall for the TV. Consider these options.

A   Behind easily movable chairs

B   A projector that can be pulled down and then put away.

C   Next to a window and off to the side

D   A Samsung Frame TV that serves as artwork above the fireplace when it's not in use.

COMMON LAYOUT CHALLENGES

THE LONG, NARROW ROOM. I like to bowl, too, but not in the living room. A long, narrow room is much harder to lay out than a square. If it has a pass-through space, it's even more difficult. Think about dividing it up with a sofa that runs perpendicular to the walls, helping break up the length. A huge mistake I see often is shoving all of the furniture against a wall, leaving a massive gap in the middle of the room. In general, a float with a walkway behind it is more inviting and intimate.

THE TOO-BIG LIVING ROOM. While no one feels sorry for those whose living rooms are too massive, it's best to try breaking it up into smaller zones for different uses. Multiple seating areas will help.

THE BACK-OF-THE-SOFA SOLUTION. Historically, it's been frowned upon to lay out a room so that you're met with the back of a sofa when you enter the space. If you can, choose two low chairs or a bench instead. That will help make the room feel more open, but if you can't avoid this, then (1) consider keeping your sofa low so it doesn't block the room visually, and (2) consider the design of the back of the sofa, using it as an opportunity to showcase something special. Budget hack: Adding a throw to the back can instantly wake up what could be a boring sofa back.

ABOVE RIGHT: The Long, Narrow Room

RIGHT: The Too-Big Living Room

OPPOSITE: The Back-of-Sofa Solution

FIND THE BEST RUG SIZE

When it comes to choosing the right size rug for the living room, I'm in the camp of "the bigger the better." Typical living room rug sizes are 8 feet by 10 feet and 9 feet by 12 feet and run the length of the sofa. As long as you have at least 8 to 12 inches between your rug and the wall, an oversize floor covering is a nice way to cozy up a space. If you have an open floor plan, it will also help you carve out the lounging/entertaining/TV-watching zone. If you can get all of the furniture to sit on the rug, great, but it's more important that every piece has the same number of legs on the rug (for example, the front legs of the sofa and the front legs of the armchair). A room will look off-balance if a sofa is squarely on a rug but the armchairs are floating off in an ocean of uncovered flooring.

Say you find the perfect rug that is too small for your space. Fear not. You can layer that beautiful vintage rug on top of a larger one like a natural jute-like rug. You can square them up or more playfully "float" the top layer if it isn't a classic rectangle shape.

OPPOSITE: Jess Bunge went for the biggest rug she could fit, adding visual space to her small apartment. The neutral grid pattern grounds the entire room.

RIGHT: A flatweave rug in a smart stripe adds a modern contrast to the traditional Chesterfield sofa and dramatic drapery.

RUGS BY THE NUMBERS

6 TO 8 INCHES: Make sure your rug is at least 6 inches wider than your sofa on both sides.

30 TO 36 INCHES: The amount of space needed as a walkway between large furniture (if your room allows for it). If not, then at least 18 to 24 inches.

8 INCHES: If you have a large enough room and want all of your furniture on your rug, then make sure you give yourself 8 inches from the edge of your furniture to the edge of your rug.

38 INCHES OR MORE: The amount of space needed between a doorframe and the rug (for a standard 36 inch door).

ADD SOME ART

Few things about making over your home can bring out all your doubts and uncertainties like trying to hang multiple pieces of art. Do you line them up? Do the frames have to match? Do they even need to be framed at all? You can certainly hang whatever you want next to whatever you want—art is almost entirely subjective, unless you're trying to sell your house, in which case your Realtor may try to tell you otherwise. But there are some things to keep in mind about *how* you hang your art.

There is the rule to keep in mind about hanging artwork around eye level, and we like it for obvious reasons, such as, it's easy to see. But your wall space doesn't always agree with us. Maybe molding keeps you from centering the piece or a sconce stands in the way. Feel free to install your piece above or below eye level.

hot tip If you don't want to put a bunch of holes in your wall, "hang" your gallery wall on art ledges or shelves.

OPPOSITE: Sometimes one or two large-scale pieces are all you need to make a statement.

ABOVE: Think outside the box with your gallery wall—don't feel like you need to stay inside a perfect square. This art layout breaks the horizontal line with a few additional pieces set below the others. Bonus: It gives the homeowner permission to keep adding to the collection.

IN THE DINING ROOM

You just need a table with chairs where you can sit and eat while trying to get your kids to chat about their day until you give up, right? Sure, designing the dining room is easier than a kitchen, and the decisions feel far less permanent, but like any room, there are ways to make sure that your formal dining room, kitchen table, or built-in banquette functions optimally and looks its best for those long dinner parties—or homework sessions.

If you have an enclosed dining room, as opposed to an open concept, this is likely one of those more temporary rooms, which means you can truly push it a little design-wise. In other words, formal doesn't have to be boring—go *grand*. Create the mood you want to have at your meals through your design, just as a posh restaurant would. This is typically a space where you can amp up the energy. One recipe for drama that I love: Make the walls pop.

But if that's too much of a commitment (or you just want to keep it simpler), you bet a paint job can make a big impact. A dark color, especially, will make your dining room the most dramatic place in the house. Plus, it's super cozy for those intimate conversations.

Corre Marie went for it and tiled the entire dining wall, creating a fresh, classic, almost coastal mood. We love how the black chairs tie in with the grout, and how the Persian rug infuses the room with color.

LEFT: Victoria Sass designed her expansive dining room with a super long table to fit the entire family and chairs comfortable enough to linger long after dinner.

RIGHT: Arlyn Hernandez designed her jewel box of a dining room with Farrow and Ball's Inchyra Blue on the walls, a custom settee with a bold pattern as a focal point, and supporting chairs and a table.

hot tip If your junction box in your ceiling isn't over your dining table, find a fixture with the wiring at one end (like Arlyn did), which will help you center the actual fixture even if the wiring is offset.

LAYING OUT THE DINING ROOM

The dining room setup is really about the size of your space and its relationship to other rooms, as well as how many people you need to seat. The shape of your room might also determine the shape of your table.

1   **FREESTANDING TABLE:** Rectangular is traditional, but go for an oval table when you need better flow (especially for pass-through dining rooms).

2   **BANQUETTE:** If you're tight on space, consider a banquette. People tend to squeeze closer than they do in chairs, and you can get away with less space between the table and wall.

3 **BEHIND THE ISLAND:** You might be tempted to add bar stools behind the island, but why not add a banquette and fit more people?

BY THE NUMBERS

SEATING FOR TWO: Go for a 24- to 30-inch square, round, or rectangular.

SEATING FOR FOUR: You'll need a 30- to 42-inch square, a 36- to 42-inch round, or a 48- to 54-inch by 30- to 40-inch rectangular table.

SEATING FOR SIX: Go big with 40 inches by 48 to 54 inches for a rectangular, or 42 to 48 inches for a round.

TYPICAL DISTANCE between the table and wall, or table and other furniture, is 30 to 36 inches. You can get away with 24 inches for stationary seating (for example, booths).

DISTANCE BETWEEN YOUR SURFACE TOP AND YOUR LIGHT SOURCE: 30 to 36 inches. This is low enough to be functional, but high enough to be out of your sightline. For a bar height island/tabletop, think 20 to 26 inches instead. You don't want your light to sit too high in the room.

CHOOSE THE PERFECT COMPANIONS

Choosing the right chairs and table is really your biggest decision in the dining room, but these days, you have *so many options* (which we covered on pages 288–289).

The good news? Your dining chairs and table do not need to match. In fact, it's a great way to bring another finish into a room that typically doesn't need too much variation.

Pay attention to the chairs' heights, though. You don't want to create an awkward human wave, with some guests sitting up high and others too low.

Got kids? Be careful about upholstery, but know that you have options:

1. A stain resistant/treated fabric (look for Crypton, Sunbrella, and Perennials brands).

2. Leather, which always cleans up nicely.

3. Vinyl can be really fun.

4. Dark and patterned fabric will hide a lot (although even milk shows up on dark linen).

5. Washable cushion covers are more work and can look messy, but they give you an option without too much commitment.

pro tip Go big with a dining room rug and allow at least 3 feet from the edge of the table to the edge of the rug, so your chairs can easily slide out without slipping off the rug.

hot tip Your head chairs can be wider than all others. You want 24-ish inches of space for each person seated. But a head chair can take up the 30 or more inches of the table's depth, so take advantage of this. The arm should fit under the table—you want 6 or 7 inches of space—but go for the cooler chair, even if it's snug.

ABOVE LEFT: A bar cart is a great addition to a dining room (should you like to imbibe).

ABOVE: The classic Saarinen tulip table is popular because of its flexibility of space and style. With only one table leg, you can fit more people and match it with many different chair styles.

BOTTOM LEFT: A dining nook doesn't have to be three-sided. A built-in upholstered bench on one side provides a lot of coziness.

ABOVE: Here's a great budget nook. Jess Bunge's dad DIY designed and built a simple structure supported with metal braces (from the hardware store) to maximize the space.

RIGHT: An island can play double duty as a prep and dining area in a small space. Just make sure it's counter height and positioned near the kitchen.

BOTTOM RIGHT: An IKEA pedestal table is elevated with four metal, wood, and leather chairs (and more can be added).

OPPOSITE: Cleo Murname created a genius kitchen table, island, and dining table in her ADU. Note the awesome double pendants that bring your eye up and don't disappoint.

SMALL-SPACE DINING ROOM TRICKS

A **BOOTH TABLE** is space saving because you need less distance between table and wall.

A **FLOATING COUNTER** can double as your dining table. Just be sure to leave space for legs and get stools that are the right height for sitting (that means counter stools, not barstools—there's a difference.)

THINK MULTIFUNCTION. A fold-down or drop-leaf table can expand when you're expecting company. You can place your table against a wall if you're really in a bind.

OPT FOR SHELVES instead of a cabinet and install them near the table to keep dining necessities and fancy dishes on display (and then USE them).

GO FOR A ROUND TABLE, especially if you're carving out a dining nook in another room. The table will be easier to slip in and out of and you can use it for other activities, like for work and games night.

KEEP IT SIMPLE. Don't try to design too much or include too much furniture. Go light on textiles, skip the rug, and focus on lighting to brighten up the space.

A round tulip table,
leather chairs,
and exposed wood
bookcase add organic
touches to this
modern dining room
by Alexander Design.

pro tip Long tables can handle long pendants (or multiples), but the width should never exceed the width of the table. If a table is 36 inches wide, the light fixture shouldn't exceed 24 inches in width.

Malcolm Simmons expertly DIY'd this wall-to-wall headboard using basic materials he bought from a building supply store. Genius.

IN THE BEDROOM

Sure, your bedroom is rarely seen by strangers, but this very private room can have a huge impact on your public self. It can even change the quality of your life (for better or worse).

And, *good news,* you just reached what I can confidently say is the easiest room in the house to design. Let that sink in while you celebrate. Why is it so simple? Well, the function of this room is mostly (wink) singular: *sleep.* This is the room where comfort rules, and symmetry is gladly encouraged, thus limiting your design decisions and giving you a much-needed reprieve. But still, there are a lot of good-to-knows and even more wish-I-had-knowns. Let's retreat to the bedroom and create a space that encourages more *zzzs,* calm, and ease (whatever that might look like to you).

LAYING OUT THE BEDROOM

You don't have a billion ways to lay out the bedroom, and that's a good thing. A bed rarely "floats" in the room, and there's no question where the nightstands should go. You likely have an obvious wall to position the bed on; add some nightstands to each side, position a dresser on literally any other wall, and you're done. But that doesn't mean there aren't guidelines for space planning, tips on how to do it best, and ideas on choosing and placing things that help you get the most calm out of your space.

Not every room has the obvious "headboard wall," and sometimes a window wall makes the best sense.

BY THE NUMBERS

24 INCHES: The ideal bed clearance around all three sides of a bedroom rug. So for a queen-size bed, go for an 8 x 10 inch rug.

7 FEET: The space between the bottom of your chandelier and the floor (for ceilings over 8 feet, add 3 inches of hanging height per foot).

50 TO 60 INCHES: Space between the top of a bedside sconce and the floor.

24 TO 27 INCHES: Ideal height of a nightstand (but just keep it 5 inches higher or lower than the top of your mattress).

ONE-THIRD: Your bedside lamp should be one-third of the surface size of your nightstand. Also, you want the bottom of the shade to be around chin level when you sit upright in bed to avoid getting blinded by the bulb.

THREE-FOURTHS: A bench at the foot of the bed should be three-fourths the width of your bed (or 6 to 8 inches narrower on either side).

If you're going to position the bed in front of a window, either keep the bed low, with a platform bed, or get a slatted headboard that lets the light stream through and doesn't feel heavy. Then, float the bed a bit so your curtains or shades can still open and close.

BEDROOM LUXURIES

You technically don't need much in a bedroom, but why not treat yourself with a room that works hard so you can stay in bed a little longer?

1   **ADD A FIREPLACE:** Cozying up in your own room is a true luxury, but if you are renovating or building consider a fireplace in your bedroom. Just be sure to raise it high enough that you can see it while lying in bed.

2   **INCLUDE A SITTING AREA:** This could be a chaise, a sofa at the end of the bed, or a pair of chairs positioned to stare at a view. if you have extra space, utilize it, and no, that chair isn't just for your laundry.

3   **BUILD IN EXTRA STORAGE:** If you are customizing a bed like Dee Murphy did, consider all the ways you can add storage (just make sure any shelves like this go at the foot of the bed, not the head).

4   **INSTALL A TV (BUT HIDE IT):** While sleep experts don't recommend it, you do whatever you want in your own bedroom even if that means marathoning *Vampire Diaries*. Consider hiding it like Rosa Beltran did here, or use a TV that looks like art when turned off.

KEEP YOUR WALLS QUIET

The bedroom is where you might put your tone-on-tone skills to the test, which could mean layering different moody tones, darker colors, and many textures to make the room feel interesting and alive. Here is a gradient of calming colors to wake up to.

Painting your ceiling the same color as the walls actually makes your room look taller because your eye doesn't stop at the paint line.

Go ahead and keep it calm with white walls. Just be sure to add touches of drama elsewhere, like these hits of black in the poufs, art, and rug.

rule breaker This Sara Ruffin Costello-designed bedroom has tile on the floor, which can feel cold underfoot and not absorb sound, but I would gladly wear slippers for the rest of my life if these were my floors.

THE RIGHT RUG

Stepping off your mattress in the morning and onto a rug is a joy, but it requires some math (or in my case, a lot of measurements and taping things off) to get the right size. A too-small rug is not a felony, but it's certainly a design misdemeanor. Our advice: Place your rug so your feet land on it when you get out of bed. That's the whole point of having a rug in this room, right?

LIGHT THE BEDROOM

The bedroom requires two distinct types of lighting: overhead and ambient. But depending on how much time you spend in this room, you may also want more direct lighting: task lighting beside your bed for reading. You might want better vanity or closet lighting so you can see how you'll look head-to-toe when you step out into the world. But at night, you'll want to turn it down low with ambient light that's most useful for relaxing.

The placement of your bedroom sconces and pendants, as well as the switches and outlets for lamps, is especially important to consider sooner than later. You need to ensure that you can control your sconces while lying in bed. You don't want to have to get up, walk around the bed, and stub your toe on your husband's dumbbells just to turn off the bedside light. We had our sconce switch mapped out, the electrician missed it, and it's as annoying as you think. Save yourself the frustration.

Keep in mind that bedside lights don't have to match, sconces and pendants save space on nightstands, and they can be plugged in if you can't hardwire.

ABOVE: Mixing a sconce and a lamp gives you lighting options all night long.

RIGHT: Classic fabric shade lamps create both ambient and directional light for reading.

ABOVE LEFT: A cool sculptural lamp leans against the wall, but well within reach (while the nightstand was sacrificed).

BOTTOM LEFT: A pendant always saves on nightstand space (just be sure the switch is within reach like Tyler Karu did).

ABOVE RIGHT: For the nighttime reader, think about adding a directional sconce just for your book.

IN THE HOME OFFICE

Whether or not you commute to work or WFH, having a well-designed office in your house will keep you feeling organized and sane. I'm not promising your bills will get opened and paid on time or your novel will get finished, but it sure can help. You might compare it to how dressing in cute workout clothes will put you one step closer to actually exercising. So let's design this space to entice you to *use* it, where function is easy, your eyeballs are happy, and comfort is prioritized.

This room can lean super utilitarian for sure, but there are many ways to reinvent the typically boring workspace so that it's a wellspring of productivity and creativity. The main players that will get you there: the desk, chair, storage, and lighting. While I personally think you have a lot of flexibility here in size and style, there are some ergonomic considerations and measurements you'll want to keep in mind to help ensure your long-term comfort.

LAYING OUT THE OFFICE

You have a few options for laying out your office, and they all revolve around where you want your desk. Obviously, how you orient it in the space greatly depends on the size of your room and desk.

1 **FLOAT IT:** If your room has the space, consider pushing the desk away from the walls. This is a great solution if you have two desks—they can face each other. You don't have to position the desk in the middle of the room, either. Floating it out from a wall with enough room—25 to 30 inches—for your chair to fit will work just fine.

2 **BY THE WINDOW:** There's nothing that says "you made it in life" more than having an office with a view—even if it's one you only use occasionally, and mostly for daydreaming and bird-watching. But choosing to place a desk, especially one with a computer, in front of your window really depends on your room's natural light.

3 **AGAINST THE WALL:** The most obvious place to position your desk is likely against an empty wall. This is a great solution if you have extra office equipment to contend with that needs to be plugged in and can't float in the room. You can even expand your desk space with a corner desk. (Find a corner with a window wall and you can have it all!)

4 **AS A BUILT-IN:** If you are renovating and adding a wall of storage, or if you're short on space, consider a clever place where you can add a desk.

hot tip If your chair has wheels consider adding a low-pile rug to protect your flooring. It will also help soak up sound and add comfort and insulation.

ABOVE RIGHT: A steel desk includes clever hidden side bookcases.

ABOVE LEFT: By floating in the room, this painted vintage wicker desk creates a sculptural effect.

RIGHT: Utilize a closet for anything but coats. Here, a desk and a few shelves create an art and crafts room.

OPPOSITE TOP: A small-scale lacquer desk doubles as a vanity.

OPPOSITE BOTTOM: A clever built-in home office right off the kitchen is super convenient for taking breaks throughout the day.

BY THE NUMBERS

30 INCHES: Minimum desktop width.

15 INCHES TO 18 INCHES: Height of seat (with your feet flat, knees level with hips, and elbows bent at 90 degrees).

20 INCHES TO 26 INCHES: Height of desk, allowing enough clearance for your legs.

30 INCHES: Minimum space needed from the edge of the desk to the wall to fit a chair (if you're floating the desk with your back to the wall).

22 INCHES: Minimum height needed from top of the desktop to a floating shelf.

36 INCHES: Minimum space needed around your furniture pieces for the best flow.

A basement can be revamped to become a home office. A coat of paint, polished cement floors, and a lot of cozy textures transformed this space into an architect's home office (and escape).

DECORATE FOR INSPIRATION

Everyone's brains work differently, and your environment will influence how well you work. Try to home in on what environments inspire you so that you'll want to be your most productive self.

A FEW TIPS TO CONSIDER

BRING IN plants to help boost air quality and create a calming effect.

HANG art and photos that keep you inspired.

DISPLAY travel mementos to stay motivated (your next vacay is so close!).

INSTALL the right window treatments, for filtered light and insulation.

CHOOSE a color palette that echoes the vibe you're going for. Are you more creative (opt for brighter colors) or do you need calm (choose a more tonal palette)?

SET OUT beautiful notebooks, pads, pens, that'll make you want to sit down and get some work done. Make a statement with customized stationery that displays your initials.

CONQUER OFFICE CLUTTER

Cord management is a real menace, especially in the office. Fortunately, plenty of conduit options exist for desks that sit against a wall.

My hack for the float is controversial, but it works well! If you have a high-pile rug, run the cord down the back of one of the desk legs. (Use gaffer tape or cord clips to keep it in place.) Then make a slit in the carpet just big enough to thread the cord through. If you are renovating, have a floor plug installed. Or you can fish the cord under the rug and run it to the wall outlet.

Some desks now come with a cord cabinet that runs along the back of the desk. Use command strips to place an outlet bank on the underside of the desk to plug everything into so your cords don't have to hang down—and then wrap the excess cords using velcro cord wraps.

LIGHT THE OFFICE

While many corporate offices have ample overhead lighting, most of us still function better with a softer ambient glow in conjunction with some directional or task lighting (especially for writing). A lamp on the desk, whether directional or ambient, might be all you need to get the job done in the darker months.

Many people find that a darker office (especially one that doesn't have a lot of natural light) feels cozy and soothing, and it can create fewer distractions, especially when you need to concentrate on a screen.

hot tip Before you go all in and buy that ugly file cabinet, consider how many files you really need to hold on to. Can many of those papers be culled, shredded, and discarded; scanned and electronically filed; or else stored in pretty storage boxes? Think about it.

OPPOSITE: This desk for a graphic designer has a cord cabinet that runs along the back, gathering all the cords in one place, reducing the mess. Finally.

IN THE UTILITY ROOMS

At first glance, the laundry room and the mudroom might feel like the least sexy ways to spend your time and money renovating, but having *hyper*functional spaces will pay off in the long run. Let's design these utilitarian rooms so that you maximize the space and efficiency, and make them easy for you to use and keep clean. Fashion follows function here for sure, but we can still make these spaces desirable, I promise.

These are the rooms that you want to decorate last, when your budget is stripped. But for resale value, these are also the rooms that offer solutions to the fantasy home buyer: The promise of a more organized life. So if time and budget permit, design accordingly.

Because laundry rooms and mudrooms need to be super functional, you should take a close look at your family's personal needs for those rooms. You might want a different washer/dryer set-up (stackable instead of side by side), or more built-in storage to greet you when you walk in the back door.

THE LAUNDRY ROOM

Once relegated to the basement, I am advocating hard for the laundry room to be near the bedrooms. If you have at least two floors, install one on the floor where the clothes end up—even if it's in a closet. Here are your options.

1   **IN THE BASEMENT:** Sure. It seems like your dirty clothes belong hidden down there, plus it doesn't take up precious real estate in your main spaces.

2   **AS PART OF THE MUDROOM:** Especially for wetter climates, consider combining these two spaces so you relegate the mess to just one area. Picture this: Kids come in from rainy soccer games, strip down, and throw uniforms straight in the washer. Nice.

3 **NEAR OR IN THE KITCHEN:** It's a good solve for a small space (and a smaller household). Hide the appliances behind cabinetry or tuck them in a closet nearby, and you'll be able to easily throw dish towels and napkins in the washer, and because it's within earshot, you won't forget your wet clothes in the washer for days. Plumbing is even easier, as the washer and dryer can tie into the water and gas or electric already run to the kitchen.

4 **IN A CLOSET:** Think about putting a stacking unit in a primary closet. No more dirty socks falling out of the basket on the way to the basement. For smaller homes that don't allow for a large laundry room, a hidden laundry closet not only keeps it central for easy access, but also saves on space. Just get a solid door instead of a hollow one to reduce noise.

LET'S TALK TASKS

The job of this room is to create a space that makes it easy to sort, wash, dry, fold, or hang clothes. Without the advent of the robot housekeeper, this is still our job, so let's make it easier. Whether you're renovating, updating, or decorating this room, let's review the items that will streamline the utility.

SORTING: The years of bending over to sift through your colors to find your whites could be over if you plan well. Three different baskets under the counter make it easy to sort as you go.

WASHING: Well, you need a washer, of course. And adding a sink will make prewash or spot soaking your clothes easier. This is great, especially if this is also your cleaning closet where you might need to rinse rags or mops.

DRYING: For this you obviously need a dryer appliance, but you also need somewhere to line-dry your delicates or set out your lay-flats-to-dry.

FOLDING: Growing up we had "folding laundry" parties while we watched movies on Friday nights, but if you actually hope to fold your clothes near the dryer, give yourself a dedicated surface. This can be as simple as a butcher block or stone installed on top of the appliances, or if you have the space, go ahead and spread out.

HANGING: For maximum efficiency, go straight from dryer to hanger by installing a rod to keep wrinkles at bay. Then you can quickly transfer the items to your closet.

IRONING BOARD: Whether you build this into a shallow closet, hang it over a door, or keep it tucked away until you need to fold it out, find an ironing board style that you'll get excited about using when it comes time to press and steam your shirts.

CLEANING AND PRODUCT STORAGE: It's always a struggle to find the balance between keeping cleaning products put away and easily accessible. Find pretty baskets, storage containers, and jars to corral detergents, dryer sheets, and sprays—whether you store them in a cabinet or on a tray that sits on your appliances.

BONUS STORAGE: You may also want a good place for all those bulky household items, like the broom, mop, or step ladder.

OPPOSITE LEFT: A simple surface and a mounted rod allow for sorting, line drying, folding, and hanging clothes.

OPPOSITE TOP RIGHT: A small sink and baskets of washcloths allow for pre-treating stains and washing delicates.

OPPOSITE BOTTOM RIGHT: A stylish tray on top of the washer corrals laundry essentials and keeps the space looking neat.

THINGS TO CONSIDER

1. What is the ideal laundry hook-up height and location?

2. Do you want a front- or top-loading washer?

3. Should the washer and dryer be stacked or sit side by side?

4. What size washer and dryer do you need?

5. Have you double-checked the dimensions and clearances of your appliances?

6. Do you have at least 6 inches allowance for dryer ventilation?

7. How much more storage do you need?

An upstairs laundry room fits snugly into a hall closet. With a wallpapered backdrop and aesthetically pleasing accessories, it's just as pretty to show off as it is to shut away.

hot tip If you have no room for extra storage, look for pedestal drawers that sit beneath front-loading washers and dryers.

THE MUDROOM

One of my favorite quotes is *"Without a system there will be chaos,"* and this applies to virtually every aspect of my life, especially the mudroom.

Homeowners of older homes lament the invention of the mudroom—it taunts and teases with its luxurious functionality. To have a designated place to hang coats, remove shoes, and drop bags, not to mention add extra storage for pantry items, pet supplies and leashes, and even a "flower cutting station" is the most uninteresting of all the renovation luxuries, but one that I want so badly. Mudroom porn is a thing for a reason.

So where do you add the mudroom?

The mudroom should be located through a side or kitchen door (not your front door), so that you can hide all the inevitable mess with easy access to your garage or driveway. Ideally it would be between the garage and the house to avoid bringing any mess further into your home.

CHOOSE THE FLOORING

Go for something that's easy to wipe clean. If you live in a really wet climate with a lot of snow that can melt, then you'll want stone or tile. Mudroom flooring is not that dissimilar from kitchen flooring, except that it'll see a lot more of inside-outside traffic and wear and tear from shoes.

OPPOSITE: My ideal mudroom has room for everything: baskets and jars, hooks for hanging coats and bags, and a bench that's high enough to store my tallest wellies beneath it.

INCLUDE PLENTY OF STORAGE

Having a place to stash your stuff is crucial, and good news, you have a lot of ready-made, DIY, or custom options. Also here is your chance to say the word *cubby* a lot, which I find fun. You can enclose the cabinetry or leave it open for easy access, or do a combination of both.

While having a proper closet with hangers is a good-to-have, make your life easier by installing sturdy hooks for heavy bags and coats that are worn every day (kids are far more likely to throw their coats on hooks than hang them up).

You also need a way to neatly store shoes you constantly put on and take off. I believe in bins and baskets stored in the cubbies so you can just throw them in without trying to carefully place and style each pair of shoes. And make sure your cubbies are tall enough to house knee-high rain boots (14 to 16 inches is a comfortable height for sitting and will allow room underneath the bench for most tall boots).

pro tip If renovating, consider adding a wash station for muddy boots and paws. Make sure the sink countertop is nonporous and super durable, so it won't scratch or stain. Alternatively, you could install a shallow powder room for washing up, or, if you're short on space, a corner slop sink or small corner shower pan with a lower faucet.

BY THE NUMBERS

5 FEET: The ideal width of a mudroom, which will give you room for a spacious bench and/or row of cabinets or lockers that measure 2 feet deep and a 3-foot hallway, allowing two people to enter the house together or one person and a few pets.

4 FEET: If space is limited, then go for a small mudroom. Plan for a 1-foot-wide drop zone, with a set of base cubbies that measure 1-foot in depth instead of a bench. The hallway should still be 3 feet wide.

12 INCHES: The space between coat hooks. You need enough space to allow wet garments to dry.

18 INCHES: Height of a bench. You'll want the depth to be 18 inches to 24 inches and the width should be 24 inches to 36 inches, which will allow for one person to sit down and remove or put on shoes.

54 INCHES TO 60 INCHES: Height of the hooks for a coatrack; adjust upward as needed to at least around eye level—around 5 feet, 6 inches—to make sure that there's enough space for coats to hang if there is a bench right below it.

12 INCHES: Minimum depth of upper cabinets. If you're adding uppers above a bench, make sure the bench is 6 inches deeper than the uppers, to avoid accidental head collisions.

RESOURCES

When it comes to shopping for your home (whether for renovation supplies or decor), you have a million options. So here is a list of design companies that I love, whose quality I trust, and many have been in my own homes (check out my blog for a list we'll keep updated as we continue to design and shop for our projects).

FLOORING

Cali Bamboo / calibamboo.com
Dinesen / dinesen.com/en
Goby Walnut / gobywalnut.com
Hallmark Floors / hallmarkfloors.com
Hewn / hewn.com
Ross Alan Reclaimed /
    rossalanreclaimed.com
Stuga / stugastudio.com/
Zena Forest / zenaforest.com

TILES

Ann Sacks / annsacks.com
Artistic Tile / artistictile.com
BuildDirect / builddirect.com
Cle Tile / cletile.com
Fireclay Tile / fireclaytile.com
Floor & Decor / flooranddecor.com
Granada Tile / granadatile.com/en/
Mission Stone & Tile /
    missionstonetile.com
Pratt + Larson / prattandlarson.com
Tile Bar / tilebar.com
The Tile Shop / tileshop.com

FIREPLACES

Electric Fireplaces Depot /
    electricfireplacesdepot.com
Heat & Glo / heatnglo.com

Starfire Direct / starfiredirect.com
Woodland Direct / woodlanddirect.com

WINDOWS, DOORS, AND TRIM

Andersen Windows /
    andersenwindows.com
Glo Windows / glowindows.com
Marvin / marvin.com
Metrie / metrie.com
Milgard / milgard.com
Sierra Pacific Windows /
    sierrapacificwindows.com
Simpson Door Company /
    simpsondoor.com
Velux / veluxusa.com

CABINETS

Boxi by Semi-Handmade /
    boxibysemihandmade.com
CliqStudios / cliqstudios.com
Dunsmuir Cabinets / dcabinets.com
Koak Design / koakdesign.com/home
Kokeena / kokeena.com
Naked Doors / nakeddoors.com
Nieu Cabinet Doors /
    nieucabinetdoors.com
Norse Interiors / norseinteriors.com
Reform / reformcph.com/us
Semihandmade / semihandmade.com
Stoffer Home /
    stofferhomecabinetry.com
Super Front / superfront.com
Unique Kitchen and Bath /
    uniquekitchenbathus.com

APPLIANCES

Aga / agarangeusa.com
Bertazzoni / us.bertazzoni.com/
Bluestar / bluestarcooking.com
Build with Ferguson / build.com
Cafe Appliances / cafeappliances.com/

Ferguson / Ferguson.com
Frigidaire / frigidaire.com
ILVE / ilveusa.com
Kohler / us.kohler.com/us/
La Canche / lacanche.com
La Cornue / lacornue.com/en-GB
Marvel / marvelrefrigeration.com
Smeg / smeg.com
Sub Zero / subzero-wolf.com
Viking / vikingrange.com

PAINT

Backdrop / backdrophome.com/
Behr / behr.com/consumer
Benjamin Moore / benjaminmoore.com
Clare / clare.com
Farrow & Ball / farrow-ball.com/en-us
Kilz / kilz.com
Portola Paints & Glazes /
    portolapaints.com
Sherwin-Williams /
    sherwin-williams.com

STONE

Artistic Tile / artistictile.com
Bedrosians / bedrosians.com
Caesarstone / caesarstoneus.com
Cambria / cambriausa.com
Pental Quartz / pentalquartz.com
Stone Universe Inc. / suistone.com

FABRIC

AphroChic / aphrochic.com
Blockshop Textiles /
    blockshoptextiles.com
Calico Corners / calicocorners.com
Caroline Cecil / carolinececiltextiles
    .com
Crypton / crypton.com
Fabric.com / fabric.com
House of Hackney /
    houseofhackney.com

Loom Decor / loomdecor.com
Mood Fabrics / moodfabrics.com
Rebecca Atwood / rebeccaatwood.com
Spoonflower / spoonflower.com
Sunbrella / sunbrella.com
Tonic Living / tonicliving.com
Zack+Fox / zakandfox.com

FURNITURE AND MORE

Ali Sandifer / alisandifer.com
AllModern / allmodern.com
Amsterdam Modern /
    amsterdammodern.com
Anthropologie / anthropologie.com
Apt2B / apt2b.com
Article / article.com
Barnaby Lane / barnabylane.com
Big Daddy's Antiques / (310) 769-6600
Burke Decor / burkedecor.com
CB2 / cb2.com
Chairish / chairish.com
Cisco Home / ciscohome.net
City Home / cityhomedpx.com
Clad Home / cladhome.com
Claude Home / claudehome.com
Crate & Barrel / crateandbarrel.com
Croft House / crofthouse.com
Design Within Reach / dwr.com
Dims / dims.world
DOMAIN by Laura Hodges Studio /
    domainbylaurahodgesstudio.com
Dressing Rooms Interiors /
    dressingroomsinteriorsstudio.com
Eclectic Goods / eclecticgoods.com
English Farmhouse Furniture /
    englishfarmhousefurniture.com
Ethnicraft / ethnicraft.com
Etsy / etsy.com
Everything But the House / ebth.com
Ferm Living / fermliving.com
Fernweh Woodworking /
    fernwehwoodworking.com
54kibo / 54kibo.com
Finnish Design Shop /
    finnishdesignshop.com
1stDibs / 1stdibs.com
Floyd Home / floydhome.com

45 Three Modern /
    @45threemodernvintage on
    Instagram
The Good Mod / thegoodmod.com
Goodee / goodeeworld.com
HAY / us.hay.com/
HD Buttercup / hdbuttercup.com
HedgeHouse / hedgehousefurniture
    .com
Home by Be / homebybe.com
Horne / shophorne.com
IKEA / ikea.com/us/en/
Industry West / industrywest.com
Interior Define / interiordefine.com
Jayson Home / jaysonhome.com
Jomo Furniture / jomofurniture.com
Jonathan Adler / jonathanadler.com
Jungalow / jungalow.com
Kaiyo / kaiyo.com
Katy Skelton / katyskelton.com
Kontrast / shopkontrast.com
Lawson-Fenning / lawsonfenning.com
Lichen / lichennyc.com
Living Spaces / livingspaces.com/
Lostine Home Goods / lostine.com
Lulu and Georgia / luluandgeorgia.com
Maiden Home / maidenhome.com
Marie Burgos Collection /
    marieburgoscollection.com
McGee & Co / mcgeeandco.com
Minted / minted.com
Neighbor / hineighbor.com
Nickey Kehoe / nickeykehoe.com
Norell / norellfurniture.com
One Kings Lane / onekingslane.com
Outer / liveouter.com
Overstock.com / overstock.com
Pamono / pamono.com
Pottery Barn / potterybarn.com
Rejuvenation / rejuvenation.com
Restoration Hardware / rh.com
Room & Board / roomandboard.com
Rove Concepts / roveconcepts.com
Sabai Design / sabai.design
Schoolhouse Electric / schoolhouse.com
Serena & Lily / serenaandlily.com
Shoppe by Amber Interiors /
    shoppe.amberinteriordesign.com

Sixpenny / sixpenny.com
Soho Home / sohohome.com
Stori Modern / storimodern.com
Studio Lani / studio-lani.com
Target / target.com
The Citizenry / the-citizenry.com
Thos. Moser / thosmoser.com
TRNK NYC / trnk-nyc.com
Urban Outfitters / urbanoutfitters.com
Wayfair / wayfair.com
West Elm / westelm.com
Woodward Throwbacks /
    woodwardthrowbacks.com
World Market / worldmarket.com

LIGHTING

Allied Maker / alliedmaker.com
Apparatus Studio / apparatusstudio.com
Brendan Ravenhill /
    brendanravenhill.com
Cedar and Moss / cedarandmoss.com
Circa Lighting / circalighting.com
Delightfull / delightfull.eu/usa
Gantri / gantri.com
Horne / shophorne.com
Hudson Valley Lighting /
    hudsonvalleylighting.hvlgroup.com
HumanHome / humanhome.co
Jones Country Road /
    jonescountyroad.com
Lamps Plus / lampsplus.com
Lamps.com / lamps.com
One Forty Three / onefortythree.com
Park Studio LA / parkstudiola.com
Schoolhouse Electric / schoolhouse.com
Shades of Light / shadesoflight.com
Starlight Lighting / starlightlighting.ca
Triple Seven / triplesevenhome.com
The Urban Electric Co. /
    urbanelectric.com
Workstead / workstead.com

RUGS AND CARPETING

ABC Carpet & Home / abchome.com
Annie Selke / annieselke.com
Armadillo Rugs / usa.armadillo-co.com
Ben Soleimani / bensoleimani.com
Beni Rugs / benirugs.com

Blue Parakeet Rugs / blueparakeetrugs.com
Corre Marie / corremarie.com
Esmaili Rugs / esmailirugs.com
John Derian / johnderian.com
Loloi / loloirugs.com
Nordic Knots / nordicknots.com
Revival Rugs / revivalrugs.com/
The Rug Company / therugcompany.com
Ruggable / ruggable.com
Rugs Direct / rugs-direct.com
Rugs USA / rugsusa.com
Stark / starkcarpet.com

WINDOW TREATMENTS

Calico / calicocorners.com
Decorview / decorview.com
Everhem / everhem.com
Hartmann&Forbes / hartmannforbes.com
Wovn Home / wovnhome.com

BED LINENS/PILLOWS

Bolé Road Textiles / boleroadtextiles.com
Boll & Branch / bollandbranch.com
Brooklinen / brooklinen.com
Caroline Cecile Textiles / carolinececiltextiles.com
Coyuchi / coyuchi.com
Cultiver / cultiver.com
Filling Spaces / fillingspaces.com
In Bed / inbedstore.com
Jillian Rene Decor / jillianrenedecor.com
John Derian / johnderian.com
Kip&Co / kipandco.com
Linoto / linoto.com
Louise Gray / louisegray.com
Magic Linen / magiclinen.com
Minna Goods / minna-goods.com
Parachute / parachutehome.com
PillowsByElissa / etsy.com/shop/PillowsByElissa
Pom Pom at Home / pompomathome.com
Rebecca Atwood / rebeccaatwood.com

Tonic Living / tonicliving.com
Tuft & Needle / tuftandneedle.com
xN Studio / xnasozistudio.com

TABLETOP

Artilleriet artilleriet.se/en/
East Fork / eastfork.com
Estelle Colored Glass estellecoloredglass.com
Ferm Living / fermliving.com
Food52 / food52.com
Grey Remedy / greyremedy.com
Hawkins New York / hawkinsnewyork.com
Heath Ceramics / heathceramics.com
John Derian / johnderian.com
Lolly Lolly Ceramics / lollylollyceramics.com
Lost & Found / lostandfoundshop.com
Material / materialkitchen.com
Nur Ceramics / nurceramics.com
Sheldon Ceramics / sheldonceramics.com
The White Company / thewhitecompany.com

FRAMES

Artifact Uprising / artifactuprising.com
Frame It Easy / frameiteasy.com
Framebridge / framebridge.com
Simply Framed / simplyframed.com

MISCELLANEOUS DECOR

Aleph Geddis / alephgeddis.com
Ben Medansky / benmedansky.com
Black Pepper Paperie Co. / studiobppco.com
BLK MKT VINTAGE / blkmktvintage.com
Bloomist / bloomist.com
Carmen Ellis Studio / carmenellis.com
Ecovibe / ecovibestyle.com
Effortless Composition / effortlesscomposition.com
Ferm Living / fermliving.com
Forbes & Lomax / forbesandlomax.com
The Little Market / thelittlemarket.com

Mantel / mantelpdx.com
Matilda Goad / matildagoad.com
Moebe / moebe.dk
Nickey Kehoe / nickeykehoe.com
sampleHAUS / mysamplehaus.com
Virginia Sin / virginiasin.com

WALLPAPER

Bien Fait / bien-fait-paris.com
Chasing Paper / chasingpaper.com
Cole & Son / cole-and-son.com
Farrow & Ball / farrow-ball.com/en-us
House of Hackney / houseofhackney.com
Hygge & West / hyggeandwest.com
Juju Papers / jujupapers.com
Kelly Wearstler / kellywearstler.com/wallpaper
Rebel Walls / rebelwalls.com
Sandberg Wallpaper / sandbergwallpaper.com
Schumacher / fschumacher.com
Sheila Bridges / sheilabridges.com
Tempaper / tempaper.com
Wallpaper Direct / wallpaperdirect.com/us
Walnut Wallpaper / walnutwallpaper.com
Yaël & Valérie / yaeletvalerie.com

ACKNOWLEDGMENTS

It's a joke around my office and at home how often I say, "Many hands make light the work." I think it's a biblical reference, but at this point I don't know where I picked it up. What I *do* know is that there were many, many, many hands that worked on this book, and trust me, it still wasn't light work for anyone.

Let's start with my former EHD team: Velinda Hellen who produced and styled most of the new original photography, curated the artists, reached out to all the homeowners and designers, and helped research and write so much of this book. She is now running her own design firm (HIRE HER!) with two former EHD members (Hi, Julie and Grace), who *also* worked on this book in the earlier stages. Thank you, Velinda—all your many skills and talents were so utilized and appreciated, and this book truly wouldn't exist without you. Next up, Sara Ligorria-Tramp, photographer and wonderful human being. After five and a half years being on my EHD team, Sara is now shooting interiors everywhere, and she's killing it. I'm endlessly grateful for her talent, skills, creativity, and professionalism. Sara, I love you and I'm proud to call you a friend and colleague. But it wasn't just those two: Erik Kenneth Staalberg, Emily Edith Bowser, Hina Mistry, Shade Tramp, Julie Rose, Grace de Asis, Veronica Crawford all helped style, research, write, edit, and hold my hand.

Of course, we need to acknowledge my editor, Angelin Borsics, who has been with me since *Styled* and without her this book would take four more years and be 900 pages. True story—my first draft was around 900 pages, so editing this down to a digestible renovation book was not an easy challenge. Angelin, I appreciate the heck out of you and am so grateful for your expertise (and your patience, kindness, and firm direction). I felt pushed and yet loved. To the rest of the incredible Clarkson Potter team who brought their A-game to *The New Design Rules*, especially Kim Tyner for her expert eyes in proofing the color, Joyce Wong, for keeping up with all the edits and evolutions this book has gone through, and La Tricia Watford, for bringing vision and beauty to the pages. Lastly, to Jenny Beal Davis, for refining the design as this book progressed. Thank you.

And writer Jessica Cumberbatch Anderson, coming into this project midway, with 900 pages of my *very important thoughts* was also a challenge (not to mention doing it through Covid), thank you for jumping in and siphoning my thoughts, while bringing another perspective to this project.

Lastly, I want to triple thank all the homeowners, interior designers, photographers, and artists who welcomed us into their homes and projects, and whose work represents extreme creativity and talent. I've learned so much from their work and have loved their bravery and rule breaking—it's totally inspiring. Please go to the credits page and follow them, hire them, and appreciate them as I do. I feel so lucky to have worked with so many talented members of our community who let their work grace these pages. THANK YOU.

DESIGN AND PHOTOGRAPHY CREDITS

We'd like to thank the following designers, as well as the photographers, stylists, and artists for allowing us to include their work. A special thanks to the homeowners for opening their doors to us.

Photography by Sara Ligorria-Tramp except where otherwise noted.

- Alexander Design; photography by Tessa Neustadt: 245 (bottom left), 294, 302 (right).
- Alli Tucker Fisher; styling by Kate Flynn: 79 (top left), 233, 246, 310 (left).
- Allison Pierce; styling by Velinda Hellen and Erik Kenneth Staalberg: 55, 74 (left), 82 (bottom), 185 (right), 222 (left), 192 (left), 251, 322 (right).
- Annie Segal and Marieke Ochtman, partners of ASOM HOME; styling by Velinda Hellen, Emily Edith Bowser, and Julie Rose; art by Minimalist Design Company, Emily Keating Snyder, Emily Ruth Design, and Stephanie Kurth: 97, 104 (left), 104 (right), 129, 157, 184 (left), 139 (left), 156, 245 (top left), 250 (left), 271, 290 (bottom).
- Arlyn Hernandez: 72 (right), 99 (left), 164, 287 (right).
- Ashley Coelho; styling by Velinda Hellen and Erik Kenneth Staalberg; art by Christina Kwan, Elissa Barber, Brittany Deupree, Nikol Wikman, Stephanie Kurth, and Ren Vois: 21, 33 (right), 38 (bottom), 61, 118 (bottom), 171, 180, 196 (middle).
- André Vippolis and Barrett Prendergast; styling by Emily Edith Bowser: 193 (right), 232 (bottom), 197 (right).
- Ben Medansky; styling by Velinda Hellen and Erik Kenneth Staalberg; art by Ben Medansky and Jones County Road: 34 (left), 66, 240 (top right), 279, 122–123.
- Bonnie and Mindy Rae; styling by Velinda Hellen and Erik Kenneth Staalberg: 48 (left), 82 (top), 98 (left), 175 (top left).
- Brady Tolbert: 70 (bottom), 88 (bottom), 92, 142 (top), 281, 315 (right).
- Carly Waters Style; styling by Velinda Hellen; art by Filling Spaces, Jamie Tubbs Studio, and Stacey Elaine: 45 (left), 53, 72 (left), 192 (right), 234 (bottom right), 247, 250 (bottom right), 210 (left), 278 (top), 304 (bottom right).
- Christa Martin; styling by Velinda Hellen and Erik Kenneth Staalberg; art by Christa Martin and Amy Jo Diaz: 28 (bottom right), 106 (right), 117 (bottom left), 154, 216, 138 (right), 194 (top right), 307 (top left).
- Claire Campbell for Mint Home Decor; homeowner Andie Macdowell: 42 (left), 254.
- Project M Plus; homeowner Cleo Murnane; styling by Velinda Hellen and Emily Edith Bowser; art by Shawn Shafer of Bison Alley, Stephanie Kurth, Jane Denton, and Renee Anne: 56, 207 (left), 293.
- Corbett Tuck; styling by Velinda Hellen, Erik Kenneth Staalberg, Emily Edith Bowser, and Julie Rose: 58, 73 (left), 80 (bottom left), 84 (top), 91, 111, 115, 117 (top left), 125 (left), 134–135, 147 (top), 221 (top right), 194 (bottom right), 212 (left), 223 (right), 231, 240 (bottom right), 242, 261, 266, 282 (right), 295, 300 (right).
- Corre Marie Larkin; styling by Velinda Hellen and Emily Edith Bowser; art by Filling Spaces, Leslie Lewis Sigler, and Elissa Barber: 109 (left), 142 (bottom), 163 (top), 176, 221 (top left), 191 (left), 286.
- Dee Murphy of Murphy Deesign; styling by Velinda Hellen: 54 (top right), 80 (top right), 87 (top), 100 (left), 145, 174, 181 (top left), 181 (top right), 248, 256 (top), 277, 288 (left), 289, 291 (right); photography by Zeke Ruelas: 224 (top), 239, 301 (left). Other project:
  - Brittany Henley VanMatre of The Spin & Give: 141 (left), 238, 323 (left).
- Emily Edith Bowser: 44 (right), 76 (right), 88 (top), 108 (right), 273, 276 (middle), 288 (right), 313 (top right).
- Emily Henderson Design:
  - Annie Segal's closet by Julie Rose: 312 (bottom right).
  - Brittany Shaw's home by Ginny Macdonald; photography by Zeke Ruelas: 94, 186 (right), 310 (right), 315 (left).
  - Chandler Tuck's home by Julie Rose: 70 (top).
  - Dan Apple's home by Ginny Macdonald; photography by Tessa Neustadt: 44 (left), 52, 100 (right), 149, 272 (left, right), 278 (bottom).
  - Holly and Ruben's home by Ginny Macdonald; photography by Tessa Neustadt: 304 (bottom right).
  - Mountain House by Emily Henderson, Julie Rose, Velinda Hellen, and Grace De Asis; styling by Emily Edith Bowser and Erik Kenneth Staalberg: 6, 37 (bottom), 48 (right), 73 (right), 107 (bottom left), 116 (bottom), 121, 124 (left), 160 (right), 159, 181 (bottom left, bottom right), 184 (right), 223, 190 (left), 197 (bottom left), 240 (left), 244 (bottom), 209 (right), 256 (bottom), 260, 214–215, 305, 316, 317.
  - Nicole and Howard Lorey's home:
    - design by Julie Rose: 62 (top right), 313 (top left)
    - design by Ginny Macdonald; photography by Zeke Ruelas: 201.
  - Oberlin Project by Emily Henderson; photography by Zeke Ruelas; styling by Scott Horne: 170, 320, 326 (all).
  - Portland by Emily Henderson, Brady Tolbert, Julie Rose, and Velinda Hellen; styling by Brady Tolbert

and Emily Edith Bowser: 13, 31, 40 (bottom), 42 (right), 62 (left), 63, 75 (right), 78 (bottom), 79 (top right), 80 (top left), 99 (right), 106 (left), 107 (right), 126 (top), 126 (bottom), 127, 148, 150 (left), 151 (right), 163 (bottom), 195, 203, 204 (left, right), 205, 212, 221 (bottom left), 228 (all), 229, 236 (right), 241, (right), 253 (top, middle), 259, 284, 300 (left), 322 (left), 325 (all), 329 (right).

- Suzanne Thune's home: 29, 60, 96, 131 (top left).
- Waverly by Emily Henderson and Ginny Macdonald: 2, 22–23, 64–65, 77, 87 (bottom), 128 (right), 182 (bottom), 253 (bottom), 276 (bottom right), 289 (right). Photography by Ryan Liebe: 79 (bottom), 98 (right). Photography by Tessa Neustadt: 114 (middle), 141 (right), 262 (top), 298–299.
- Erica Reitman; styling by Velinda Hellen and Erik Kenneth Staalberg: 146, 182.
- Erik Staalberg: 101.
- Ginny Macdonald: 45 (right), 85, 144 (bottom right). Additional projects:
  - Esther and Seong Kim's home: 107 (top left), 124 (right), 202 (top), 225, 227, 257.
  - Jaclyn Johnson and David Kaul's home; styling by CJ Sandgren: 39, 183, 186 (left), 193 (left), 234 (top right), 264 (left).
- Jamie Haller; restoration by Jamie Haller and Craig Ekedahl; styling by Velinda Hellen; art by 100x Better: 117 (right), 118 (top), 120, 130, 175 (right), 241 (left), 252, 265, 312 (left).
- Jayma Mays and Adam Campbell; styling by Emily Edith Bowser and Erik Kenneth Staalberg; art by Stephanie Kurth: 19, 32 (right), 50 (right), 125 (right), 131 (bottom left), 143, 152 (right), 153, 161 (right), 169 (left), 191 (right), 208 (left), 290.
- Jess Bunge: 17, 69, 147 (bottom), 194 (left), 234 (left), 280, 292 (top left).
- Julie Rose: 62 (right), 304 (left), 313 (top right). Art by Elissa Barber on pages 62 and 313.

- Kassina Folstad of Hello Norden; photography by Belen Fleming: 236 (bottom left), 211 (left).
- Keyanna Bowen; photography by Keyanna Bowen: 311 (left).
- Lea Johnson; photography by Sage E Imagery: 68 (bottom).
- Malcolm Simmons of Mas Means More; photography by Keyanna Bowen: 60 (right), 296.
- Michael Keck: 160.
- Nine Arrows Lake House; styling by Emily Edith Bowser and Erik Kenneth Staalberg: 41, 60 (left), 131 (right), 150 (right), 208 (right), 275, 291 (bottom left).
- Rashida Banks; photography by Keyanna Bowen: 140 (right).
- Rosa Beltran Design; styling by Velinda Hellen; art by Ninos Studio, Stephanie Kurth, Angela Chrusciaki Blehm, and Shawn Shafer of Bison Alley: 50 (left), 74 (right), 78 (top), 80 (bottom right), 151 (right), 190 (right), 213, 199 (bottom), 289 (left), 308.
- Sarah Zachary of Zachary-Jones Studio; homeowners Kitt and Yoni Fife: 33 (left), 49 (left). Additional projects:
  - Styling by Emily Edith Bowser: 71, 173, 197 (top left).
  - Lauren and Ari Taitz's home: 70 (middle).
- Sara Ligorria-Tramp; homeowners Eric Tramp and Ana Ligorria-Tramp: 38 (top).
- Sara Ruffin Costello; styling by Velinda Hellen and Erik Kenneth Staalberg: 4, 30, 34 (right), 37 (top), 43, 49 (right), 75 (left), 86, 105 (left), 119, 171, 244 (top), 206 (left), 209 (left), 264 (right), 303, 307 (right).
- Scott Horne; styling by Velinda Hellen and Erik Kenneth Staalberg: 9, 105 (right), 158 (top), 276 (left), 283, 306 (bottom): 76 (left), 207 (right).
- Shaun Crha of Wrensted Interiors: 187 (bottom), 206 (right).
- Sherry Shirah; styling by Velinda Hellen and Erik Kenneth Staalberg: 32 (left), 35, 68 (top).

- Spaulding Company; homeowners Erin and Aaron Bruno; photography by Lily Glass: 224 (bottom).
- Tyler Karu; photography by Justin Levesque: 144 (top right). Photography by James Salomon: 307 (bottom left).
- Valerie Legras Atelier; styling by Velinda Hellen and Erik Kenneth Staalberg: 116 (top), 311 (right), 313 (bottom left).
- Velinda Hellen Design: 90, 108 (left), 136, 137 (top, bottom), 196 (top), 202 (bottom), 292 (top right). Photography by Veronica Crawford: 222 (top right), 304 (top right). Additional project:
  - Meredith and Oliver Riley Smith's home; styling by Emily Edith Bowser: 11, 57, 83, 144 (left), 188, 189, 222 (bottom right), 232 (top), 236 (top left).
- Velinda Hellen and Sara Ligorria-Tramp; homeowners Sara Ligorria-Tramp and Macauley Johnson; art by Stephanie Kurth: 28 (top right), 84 (bottom), 132 (left), 152 (left), 159 (left), 168 (right), 175 (bottom left), 185 (left), 200 (left), 220, 268, 269, 291 (top left); styling by Emily Edith Bowser: 318.
- Victoria Sass of Prospect Refuge Studio; photography by Wing Ho: 112, 162, 170 (right), 219, 237, 287 (left). Photography by Amanda Marie Birnie: 114 (bottom). Additional project:
  - Nancy Zeis's home; photography by Amanda Mari Birnie: 128 (left), 249.
- William Hunter Collective; styling by Velinda Hellen, Erik Kenneth Staalberg, Emily Edith Bowser, and Julie Rose: 26, 36, 40 (top), 46, 95, 109 (right), 114 (top), 139 (right), 163 (middle), 166, 167, 200 (right), 211 (right), 230, 245 (top right), 250 (top right), 263, 274 (bottom right), 292 (bottom right), 302 (left), 312 (top right), 314, 319, 323 (right).